Golf Magazine's
SHORTCUTS
to Better Golf

Golf Magazine's
SHORTCUTS
to Better Golf

Edited by Lew Fishman and

the Editors of
Golf Magazine

Illustrations by Dom Lupo &
Lealand Gustavson

Galahad Books · New York

Published in 1993 by

Galahad Books
A division of Budget Book Service, Inc.
386 Park Avenue South
New York, NY 10016

Galahad Books is a registered trademark of Budget Book Service, Inc.

Published by arrangement with Harper Collins Publishers, Inc.

Library of Congress Catalog Card Number: 78-19559
ISBN: 0-88365-820-8

Printed in the United States of America.

Contents

3. SHOTMAKING AND TROUBLE PLAY
By Johnny Miller

4. CORRECTING THE FAULT
By Harvey Penick

7. PUTTING

8. MENTAL APPROACH

9. EXERCISE AND PRACTICE

Introduction

Through the years, countless swing theories and dissertations have inundated the hapless amateur golfer attempting to sharpen his game. This is not to say that there have been no valid contributions to golf instruction by tour stars who have sought to relate their secrets of success or by club professionals more closely associated with the teaching part of the game. However, it has been a painful process in which many golfers have been left wanting and confused.

We, the editors of *Golf Magazine,* have concluded that the most effective way to communicate with the average golfer is to leave him with one key thought on which to work. We call these Pointers, and we have published hundreds over the years. Using Pointers, we have structured this book in such a way that readers can readily identify their problems and find remedies. The format also is beneficial to the beginner who is attempting to build a strong foundation. We touch on every aspect of the game: pre-swing (address), swing, short game, sand, putting, shotmaking, curing the fault and mental approaches to playing.

This instruction represents proved techniques and methods offered to you by some of the finest thinkers in the game of golf. To round out the picture, we have included a section on exercise and practice to help you play your best golf.

The Editors

1

PRE-SWING

When top touring pros experience difficulty with their games, the first area to which they turn is the pre-swing routine, and with good reason. The fundamentals of grip, stance, posture and alignment form the foundation upon which a golf swing is built.

Although no two players execute the golf swing exactly alike, there are certain elements which can be considered axiomatic. The major reasons for deviation from this so-called norm can usually be traced to the physical characteristics of the individual players.

Let's take the grip, for example. Arnold Palmer, Sam Snead or Ben Hogan, almost every great United States champion uses or has used the Vardon grip. But Jack Nicklaus, whose hands are relatively small, is an exponent of the interlocking variety. Regardless, the function of the grip remains the same—to allow both hands to work as one unit, linking the energy of the body to the club and returning the club squarely to the ball at impact.

In the left hand, the club should run from the middle joint of the forefinger, across the bottom of the middle two fingers, to under the butt of the hand. The right-hand grip is more in the fingers, and the key here is the snugness of the fit between the left thumb and the channel between the butt and the ball of the right hand along the "lifeline."

The trademark of a good grip is that the hands should be as close as possible to each other. There should be no air between the left thumb and the lifeline of the right hand.

One way to check whether you are holding the club correctly is to take your grip, then open up your hands. Your palms should be parallel and at a right angle to the target line.

Once you have taken hold of the club, you are ready to assume your stance.

Go out to the practice tee on a Saturday morning or to a driving range, and you will be able to analyze a person's handicap just by watching him step up to the ball. Most amateurs have a tendency to hunch over the ball, reaching for it and creating a good deal of stress and discomfort in the lower back.

The proper posture and balance are attained simply by flexing the knees a bit, with the back fairly straight. If you can think of sitting on a high barstool, it might help. Once you have flexed your knees, all that remains is to bend a bit from the waist, maintaining your head in a natural position in relation to your shoulders. You should actually feel fairly erect when standing up to the ball, with your weight distributed evenly between your feet.

Another checkpoint: If you feel you have too much weight on your toes, you know you are reaching for the ball. Conversely, if you feel most of the weight is on your heels, your hands are going to be too close to the body and your swing will be cramped. Try to be as natural as possible, and allow your hands just to hang by your sides.

Good posture and address facilitate the transmission of energy from the lower body or legs to the ball. They are essential building blocks. Since it has been estimated that some 60 to 70 percent of the power derived in a good golf swing comes from the legs, you can see how important it is that you concentrate and develop the proper pre-swing habits.

As you prepare to set up to the ball, you must realize that the width of your feet is dictated by the club you are using on the particular shot. For wood shots, you can figure, as a rule of thumb, that the feet will be planted a bit wider than the width of the shoulders or at least even with the shoulders. As you move to your shorter irons, the width of the stance becomes narrower.

While the exact position varies from player to player, for the most part, it will help a golfer to have his left foot turned out toward the hole rather than toward the ball or square. If your left foot is square, it will block out your left side when you drive off your right leg and through the ball.

As regards the right foot, many players, including Ben Hogan, maintain it in a square position, but some of the younger prospects, including Ben Crenshaw, turn it away from the hole, claiming this allows them a freer shoulder turn.

The position of the right foot actually controls the action of your right leg through the swing. With the right foot turned out a bit, the right knee will give a bit at the top of the backswing, allowing a bigger and freer shoulder turn and a larger arc.

Again, as a general rule, the ball should be played opposite the left heel for all wood shots, while as you work your way down from a driver to a short iron, narrowing your stance, you will also want to move the ball back toward your right foot a bit more. This makes it easier to hit down and through the ball. One note of caution, though, and that is: Do not move the ball too far back—most amateurs need all the height on the shot that they can get.

Now that you have your weight evenly distributed between your feet, have flexed your knees and feel the tension in your thighs rather than in your lower back, have set your feet properly for the club you are using and have the ball in proper position, it is time to give thought to the position of the shoulders and hips.

Both the shoulders and the hips should be generally square—that is, parallel to the intended line of flight. In essence, the shoulders direct the arc of the swing. So if they are open, or pointing to the left at address, you will be forced to move back to the ball on an outside-in path, cutting across it. The result: a slice most of the time, sometimes a pull. If the shoulders are closed, or pointing to the right at address, the opposite will be true. You will be coming at the ball from inside-out. The result: a hook most of the time, sometimes a push, depending on the face of the club at impact.

A checkpoint when positioning the shoulders is to look downtarget over your left shoulder. It should point just a hair left of the target, parallel to the target line.

If you set your left shoulder, left arm and the club shaft in more or less of a line toward the ball, you will find the left shoulder will automatically be higher than the right. This line of the left shoulder, arm and club also gets the head and hands in correct position. It will not allow you to have your head directly over the ball or your hands too far behind it.

If your left arm is in good position, your head has to be behind it. Your hands should be just behind the ball for the driver, and more over the ball for the fairway wood and iron shots. This strong left side setup also ensures that the hips will be square. With the left arm fairly firm and the right arm a bit more passive, hanging closer to the body, you are ready to begin your backswing smoothly. Develop a routine for yourself. Enlist the aforementioned checkpoints. Build a solid foundation . . . one building block at a time.

OVERLAP—DON'T DISLODGE

I've noticed that a lot of players instinctively separate the forefinger from the other fingers of their left hands as they drape the pinkie of the right over it when they grip the club. It looks as if they are wedging the pinkie between the index finger and the forefinger, causing the knuckle of the forefinger to protrude. This is a half-interlock grip and actually dislodges the forefinger of the left hand from the grip. **Either fully interlock or keep the knuckles of the left hand together and in line on the grip.** Let the pinkie of the right hand rest on the bridge formed by the fingers of the left hand, but don't move that bridge to give it a place to snuggle into. □

BY ARNOLD PALMER

5

LET EVERY FINGER WORK FOR YOU

In accordance with the "don't knock it if you haven't tried it" philosophy, I suggest the use of the full-finger, or baseball grip, for certain golfers. I've adopted this grip after twenty-two years on the links, and find I'm hitting the ball with greater authority. Players who don't hit the ball as far as they'd like to should try it, as should older players who have lost some zip in their hand speed. Ben Hogan once said that once his left hand brought the club into the hitting position, he wished he had three right hands to hit the ball with. **The full-finger** grip retains the left hand as the prime hitting guide, and I believe it also allows the right hand more activity in the hitting area.

It's a fairly simple process. The little finger of the right hand is lifted off the index finger of the left hand, where it rides for conventional grips, and is placed on the club itself. The thumbs still point down the shaft as with the standard overlapping or interlocking grips. The "V's" of both hands remain pointed to the right shoulder. Most of the grip's pressure is kept in the first three fingers of each hand. □

BY BILL MARKHAM

SHAKE HANDS AND RELAX

Right-hand tension causes many golfers nightmares. At address this tension forces the right arm into a position too far away from the body, resulting in an outside-in swing and a slice. If the golfer would only relax and shake hands with his club, he would find his right arm would be closer to his body, which would facilitate swinging on the correct path. □

BY DAN PESANT

8

PRESS PALMS TOWARD EACH OTHER

SQUEEZE YOUR GRIP

To ensure a firm grip without creating a viselike hold on the club, **take your normal grip and then gently squeeze the two hands toward each other.** Your hands and wrists will still be flexible, and you'll be more aware of your hands working as a unit. This should be the last move before starting the swing, so that it will serve a double purpose of securing your grip and turning on your ignition. □

BY TOM FLOW

CONSTANT PRESSURE

LOOSE GRIP

Lupo

MAINTAIN YOUR GRIP

It's absolutely imperative that you hold the club firmly in the last three fingers of the left hand. It's at the top of the backswing that most golfers lose this firmness, usually because they let the club drop below a horizontal plane. **A good way to check yourself is to place a coin against the shaft under the pinkie and ring finger of the left hand.** If your grip is loosening at the top, the coin will fall out of its nook. If you're maintaining a good grip, the coin will stay entrenched. ☐

BY BILL KIDD

PRACTICE WITH FEET TOGETHER

START WITH YOUR FEET TOGETHER

Balance is one of the most important elements of the golf swing. You'll never see a good player with moving feet because a loss of balance destroys the smooth swinging action necessary to making a good shot. **To ingrain balance, practice swinging with your feet together.** You'll find that you'll eliminate excessive body movement, hit the ball almost as far as you normally would and use very little effort. The moment you lose balance it means you've overswung or tried to use too much body. As you develop rhythm and consistency, gradually spread your feet to shoulder width, but keep that same sense of balance. ☐

BY FRED AUSTIN

PRE-LOCK YOUR LEFT ARM

One of the cardinal rules of golf is "keep the left arm straight." It's also one of the more difficult concepts to master. I help my students by having them take a normal grip and address and then having them roll their left elbows in toward their bodies. This prelocks the left arm in a solid, straight position for the rest of the swing. □

BY BRIAN ANDERSON

TURN HEAD TO STAY MORE BEHIND SHOT

CHIN BACK GETS BODY BEHIND

This tip is especially for those of you who have trouble getting the ball in the air. Hitting the ball high is the key to accuracy and usually results in more distance, too. If you've ever watched Jack Nicklaus swing, you've probably noticed that he turns his head to the right before he starts his swing. **By turning the chin so that it's behind the ball, Jack helps ensure that his body will stay behind the blow and that his right shoulder will go under the chin before the head comes up—both keys to hitting the ball high.** □

BY JIM SPACH

USE TENNIS TO IMPROVE YOUR GOLF

It's often said that golf and tennis have almost nothing in common, that there is little "how-to" information you can transfer from one sport to the other. Well, here's one very important similarity. When you address a golf ball, your knees should be flexed to the same degree that they would be if you were about to return a tennis serve. Keep this picture in mind, and you'll improve your power and accuracy in both sports. □

RICK GRAVES

14

AVOID "TOE DANCING"

Getting "up on your toes" is a bad habit that causes improper balance during the swing. In most cases it results from reaching too far to the ball. To check against toe dancing, try lifting your toes when you are in the address position. If you can't lift your toes without moving another part of your body, you're reaching too far. Step closer to the ball, and stand a little taller so that your weight is distributed evenly between the balls and heels of your feet. This will improve your posture and set you up for a well-balanced swing. □

BY DONALD McDOUGALL

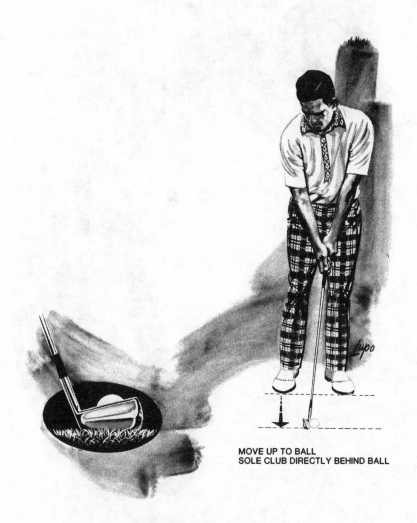

MOVE UP TO BALL
SOLE CLUB DIRECTLY BEHIND BALL

MAKE SURE THE CLUB IS SOLED

A good swing will bring the club back to where it was at address. So you're only hurting yourself if you don't set up with the club soled behind the ball in the ideal hitting position. A good exercise to implement this is to start addressing the ball from an overextended position and then to move up on the ball until the club is completely soled. You might be surprised at how close you are to the ball, but don't worry, you're finally in the right position. □

BY DOUG GRAVES

17

KEEP IMPACT IN YOUR MIND

To achieve maximum distance and accuracy, it's imperative that you strike the ball with the center of the clubface. I make sure this happens by keeping a mental picture of contact in my mind through the swing. At address, I put the center of the club up against the ball, and then imagine that I'm swinging with the ball embedded in the face of the club. **This gives my hands a precise target at impact—the return of the club to the same position it was in at address.** □

BY CLAUDE KING

LINE UP WITH AN "L"

To stress the importance of target awareness, accurate alignment and proper ball position—three things I find lacking in the average player's game—I use this mental image. I ask the player to pretend his ball is sitting on the corner of a large letter "L," formed by the target line and the line that extends from his left instep to the ball. By visualizing this "L" he can easily retain a clear perspective of the target and can align his feet and body on a line parallel to the target line. □

BY DALE SHANKLAND

Lupo

THE FOUR-STEP SETUP

Many cases of misalignment stem from a bad habit of placing the feet while looking at the ball instead of the target. With this four-step procedure to address the ball, correct alignment is guaranteed: (1) Take a preliminary stance, holding the club lightly with the right hand. Rest the club behind the ball. (2) Look at the target, and line up your feet accordingly, making sure your eyes stay on the target as you shift your feet. (3) Look from the target to the ball and back again as you line up the clubface. (4) Lastly, take your full grip, and make any necessary adjustments. Now you can swing, confident that you're aligned correctly. □

BY JOHN COWAN

2

SWING

Today more than ever, golf must be considered a power game. Likewise, the swing has evolved from an action which stressed the hands and wrists to a move which incorporates and utilizes the full power potential in the various parts of the torso.

Watching the pros consistently pound the ball 250 yards or better off the tee, you realize that if you can get your legs, shoulders, hips, arms and back into the ball in a smooth, coordinated and timed motion, you have to fly the ball farther than the person who is wasting these important power sources.

For the sake of clarity, in this chapter, we are going to study the role of each part of the anatomy during the golf swing.

First, let's look at the arms. You've always heard that the left arm must be straight in order to generate any sort of power in the swing, but perhaps you've never learned why. Without a straight left arm, it is virtually impossible to achieve what is known as the power arc, and if the left arm is bent excessively, the club cannot be pulled through on an inside-out plane because the right arm will take over and force the club outside. The arm need not be perfectly rigid, but it must be relatively straight to keep the left side firm.

It also may be a surprise to you that the "golf" muscles in the arms are not the biceps. The key muscles are those on the underside of the forearms. One look at the way these muscles bulge when Arnold Palmer grips the club will show you this. The biceps aid overall strength, but you should take care to develop those muscles in the forearms.

Now for the shoulders. There is not a single golfer on the tour who does not employ a full shoulder turn. It should be obvious, then, that this is one of the basic principles of good golf. At address, you should set up with the left shoulder slightly forward and above the right. This will let your body feel the correct movement as you swing the club.

If you take the club back properly, with the left hand or arm providing the dominant force, you should not start down until the left shoulder has moved under the chin. A good takeaway will help you reach this position. As you take your downswing, the shoulder movement is crucial. The left shoulder turns out toward the target, and the right one tucks under the chin.

The hips are used much the same as the shoulders; only the turn is not quite as radical. The most important thing to stress is the movement of the left hip at the start of the downswing. It must move laterally to initiate the action back to the ball and then turn out from the ball to allow the hands and legs to drive through.

If you fail to get the left hip moving early, the right side is blocked because you have prevented your body from completing its shift of weight. Let the hips move down the line of flight; then rotate away from the ball in unison with your legs, and you will find your timing will improve considerably. It's good timing, not simple force, that creates power. And good timing is total coordination of the proper body movements.

The legs are the factor most often overlooked. It probably is safe to say that the average golfer makes little or no use of the power potential of his legs when he plays golf. Care must be taken at address to keep the legs flexible. Stiff legs will only cause you to lose your balance. Stand up to the ball with the knees slightly bent and relaxed, and keep them that way throughout the swing.

On the backswing, the left knee should point to the ball while the right knee straightens slightly, but not completely. As you return to the hitting area, the left leg moves out toward the target and the right knee is thrust to the ball and then the target in a smooth motion. If either leg stiffens, you're out of position to hit the ball, and you've lost accuracy and distance.

As you look at the dynamics of the golf swing, you will come to realize that the left side is dominant. You begin at address by establishing the radius of your swing with the left arm, lining it up with the shaft of the club. The right arm is soft, passive; the head bent. Then the first move in the backswing accentuates this left-side dominance as the left hand, left arm, left shoulder and left leg initiate the action as a single unit. The move of the left leg actually pushes the right hip out of the way, subduing the power of the right. At the top of the swing, you will feel a tension in your left side, across the top of your back and through the triceps, but you should feel no tension of the right side. In effect you have turned your left side around your right leg.

The uncoiling of the left side sets up a pulling motion from the left side back to the ball. Feel as though the left foot and left arm start down together and as though the left side is in complete control of the swing. When you are swinging well, you will find that the right side can release as strongly as it wants. That is only because the left side is working actively through the ball. You allow the right side to release. You don't force it.

If your finish is not full, your right side developed tension at some point in the swing and took control. If this is the case, analyze the action of your legs and your feet. You should finish on the toes of your right foot and on the outside of your left—that is, if you allowed the left to act as the guide.

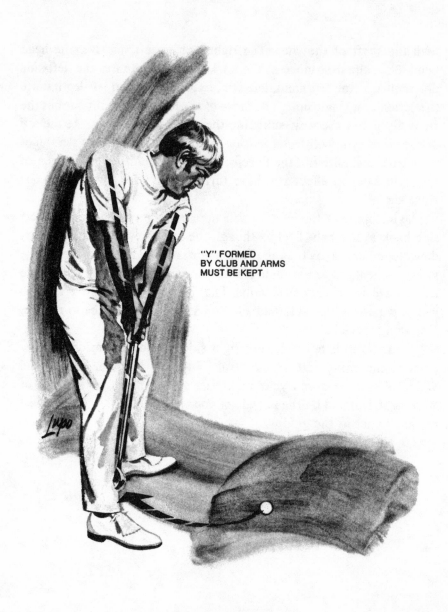

"Y" FORMED
BY CLUB AND ARMS
MUST BE KEPT

MAINTAIN YOUR "Y"

Most people concentrate on the result of the shot and pay little or no attention to the execution. This attitude leads to inconsistency. Good shots are a result of a good swing, a controlled swing that is deliberately kept along a desired path. To ensure consistency, you have to have a key that starts the swing the same way every time. My own key is the position of the shaft in relation to the arms. **I keep the butt end of the shaft pointing to the "Y" formed by my arms throughout the takeaway.** This guarantees a full extension away from the ball. If you use too much wrist action on the takeaway, the end of the club will point at the target and the "Y" (the arms plus the club shaft) will be broken. □

BY PHIL RODGERS

KEEP ON THE GRASS!

Please keep on the grass! That's what I tell my pupils to help them start back correctly. Full extension of the left arm in the backswing is vital for producing maximum arc in the swing—you will never approach full extension if you allow the right hand to pick the club up too early in the takeaway. The way to avoid an early pickup is to make the clubhead stay on the grass for the first foot or so going back. By your just brushing the clubhead along the top of the grass instead of picking it up quickly, your swing will be longer and more consistent. □

BY ROY BOWE

DRAG CLUB ON BACKSWING

TURN THAT CHEST

Every teacher agrees that a full shoulder turn is necessary for consistent golf shots. However, I have found that many pupils find it difficult to "turn their back on the hole" or "turn the left shoulder under the chin," the most common keys given to get the job done. Instead, I ask my pupils to think of turning the center of the chest away so that at the top of the swing the center of the chest faces away from the target. This image helps them make a full shoulder turn a lot more easily. □

BY RICK McCORD

PULL TO AVOID A DIP

The dipping of the left shoulder as you initiate the backswing gives a false sense of turning. You want to turn away from the ball with your left shoulder, not drop it. To avoid dipping, try to pull around with the right shoulder. The left will follow without excessive dipping. This pulling action of the right shoulder will give you a fuller shoulder turn, eliminate excessive tilting of the shoulders and put the club on a slightly flatter plane, which will allow the club to extend through the line of flight longer. □

BY JIM COLBERT

LEFT THUMB
COCKED AND
POINTING AT
TARGET

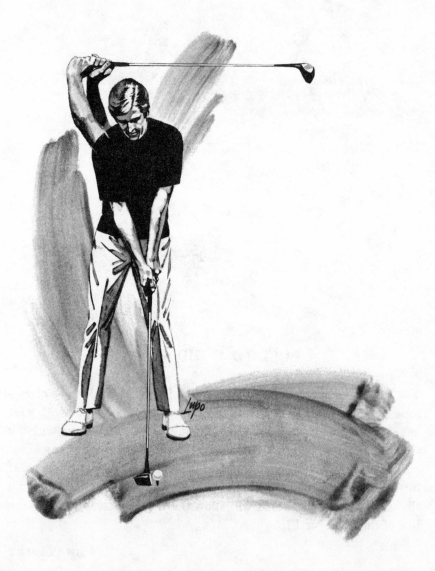

THUMB THE FLAG AT THE TOP

There's an easy way to make sure your club is horizontal at the top of the backswing. Your left thumb is a perfect guide. **At address, apply a little extra pressure to the thumb so that you'll be aware of it without really concentrating on it.** Then, at the top of the backswing, you'll feel it under the shaft and pointing at the hole. When it achieves this position, your club is horizontal and your wrists are cocked. Without your even thinking about it, this will force you to concentrate on the swing more than on bashing the ball. □

BY AL FEMINELLI

A NICE TURN OF THE ANKLES

To obtain a powerful golf swing, there must be a solid foundation, a foundation which will key the balance and timing of the swing. **Since movement of the feet must be restricted in order to prevent swaying, concentration is placed upon the ankles for turning.**

If you tried to take a full turn flat-footed, you would find it awkward and difficult. But take the same turn and roll the left ankle in toward the right foot, and it seems much more natural to take that turn.

On the downswing, the ankles again come into play in order to prevent the weight from staying on the right foot. **The left ankle rolls toward the target at the start of the downswing, and the right ankle rolls toward the target as the hands enter the hitting area.** This ensures your weight transfer and lets you finish the swing with the balance distributed on the outside of your left foot. It also gets your right foot off the ground and up on the toes, a sure sign that you've delivered a full, powerful swing. □

BY DOUG TURNESA

THINK DOWN

THINK DOWN TO HIT THE BALL UP

Many golfers have trouble with iron shots because while they are swinging at the ball, they are also thinking "up" when they should be thinking "down." Don't worry about getting the ball in the air. The iron's natural loft will do that. Your objective is to get a clean, solid hit. To do that, you must strike the ball with a descending blow. So when you swing, think "down," think about actually driving the ball down into the turf. There is no better way to get a ball up than to try to hit it down. □

BY CHARLES SAUNDERS

BUCKLE
FACES
TARGET

BUCKLE TO THE TARGET

Many golfers have trouble shifting their weight correctly in the
downswing. One good way to get your weight to the left side is to feel
that you are throwing your belt buckle at the target. This initiates the
downswing with the lower body, transfers the weight and causes the
hands to pull straight down, resulting in a late release and a high
finish. □

BY JOHN CAFONE

37

VISUALIZE A HIGH FINISH

Spectators often used to ask me how I hit the longest ball they'd ever seen. I always said it came from releasing the clubhead through the ball. But until I started teaching, I found it difficult to explain this concept. Now I tell the golfers to **forget about releasing at the bottom and think about making as high a finish as possible with the hands.** By thinking of a high finish, golfers automatically release everything at impact in order to get the hands high at the completion of the swing. This prevents quitting and helps give them all the power and distance their physiques are capable of generating. □

BY GEORGE BAYER

GHOST THE RIGHT HAND

The secret to distance and accuracy is knowing when to use the right hand. The average player hardly ever waits for the right moment but starts applying pressure with the right hand as soon as he starts into the downswing. The only time the right hand should be employed is in the hitting zone—those fifteen or so inches before and after impact. **What I suggest is that you think of the right hand as a ghost that is nonexistent at the top and slowly materializes as you move toward impact.** Keep pulling with the left hand, and let the right naturally gather its own power. You'll find it's there when you need it even though you're not really aware of its arrival. □

BY LARRY OSTRANDER

KEEP HANDS
MOVING OVER
FRONT BALL

Lupo

PLACE SECOND
BALL HERE

YOU MUST ACCELERATE

Acceleration is essential in every shot from a drive to a putt. However, making the ball the ultimate target often causes the clubhead to reach peak speed too soon, so that it actually decelerates into the impact area. To make sure you accelerate, place a ball two feet in front of the one you're hitting and directly in line with the target. Now swing, making sure that your hands lead the clubhead out over that ball without slowing down. If you aim your attention at the second ball, there'll be no slowing down, and you'll derive maximum clubhead speed from your swing. □

BY SLUGGER WHITE

SPEED THE KNEES FOR POWER

All women golfers, and most men, would get more distance if they'd speed up the tempo of their swings, especially in the lower part of the body. I try to begin my backswing with a quick weight shift to the right side. **This is accomplished by my rolling the left foot and left knee toward the right immediately.** When I get to the top, I start down by pushing off the right foot and sliding my hips directly at the target. This push throws my right knee toward the left and gives me momentum through the ball. □

BY JOANNE CARNER

LEAD WITH A FIRM LEFT

Let's say you are the offensive lineman on a football team and you are trying to hold the defensive lineman from penetrating to your quarterback. Assume the only way you could stop him was with your left forearm. The left forearm, during the golf swing, is used in the same manner at impact and through. To guide a powerful swing, lead with the left forearm during impact, just as the offensive lineman does in stopping the defensive football player. The defensive player could never stop him by merely slapping his hand at him but, like the golfer, must use his entire forearm, keeping the wrist firm throughout. □

BY GUY MOSER

42

ASSURING THE LATE HIT

To ensure the late hit that produces extra distance, the angle between
the club shaft and the left arm must be maintained for as long as
possible before impact. The best way to hold this angle is to swing
with the big muscles of the body—primarily the legs—to avoid
manipulating the club with the hands. To get the feel of this, practice

swinging the club against a medicine ball in the downswing. If you don't have a medicine ball, two old mattresses will serve the purpose. Either way, this technique will delay the release of your hands as well as strengthen your all-important left side and create the power you may have been lacking in your game. □

BY STEVE PEMBROOK

CHIN KEYS ON RIGHT SHOULDER

WAIT FOR THE RIGHT SHOULDER

A steady head position is vital if the swing is to stay within the initial arc created by the takeaway. If the head moves off the ball because you're anxious to see where the ball is going, you are destroying the flow at the most crucial moment—just before contact with the ball. **Wait for the right shoulder to pass under the chin, and let it push your head up with it as your arms complete the follow-through.** The ball will be well on its way, but you'll instinctively be able to pick up its flight. You'll also begin to notice that it's going right where you want. □

BY MIKE FITZGERALD

FULL HIP TURN

CLEAR THE LEFT HIP

There's too much talk about "driving the knees laterally" as the first move of the downswing. With most average golfers, this move blocks them entirely—the hips slide forward in the downswing, and all they can do is "push" the club at the target with stiffened arms and wrists. This "pushing" action slows the clubhead and results in loss of power. Instead, think of using the right hip to clear the left out of the way as you swing down. The left hip will turn to the left, as it should, allowing you to release strongly through the ball. □

BY BRYAN HESSAY

CLUBHEAD POINTS TO SKY
AT FULL EXTENSION

EXTEND THE CLUBHEAD TO THE SKY

You often hear the pros say they picture the shot before they hit it. What they're doing is programming their bodies to swing the club along a certain line. **A good pre-shot image for the average player is one of extending the club toward the horizon and then into the sky on his follow-through.** If you can visualize the clubhead's extension pulling your hands and body through the impact area, you'll have no trouble with off-line shots. The club will extend right up the flag into the sky, and your body will be turning to face the target. □

BY DALE DOUGLASS

3

SHOTMAKING AND TROUBLE PLAY

By Johnny Miller

When the average golfer stands on the tee, he expects to hit the ball straight down the fairway, but more often than not, he winds up hooking or slicing. Then, in the rough and needing to bend the ball around a tree or some other obstacle, he invariably hits it straight and winds up in even worse trouble.

The ability to draw or fade the ball when you want to—instead of when you don't want to—can save you many strokes, and I'll try to outline some of the shots that have helped me on the tour and will help you become a shotmaker.

Ben Hogan, whom I've studied, was such a masterful player that he could hit as many as ten different shots without ever taking his hands off the club or changing the plane of his swing. Most club golfers, however, think that for an intentional fade, draw, hook or slice, their swing plane has to be changed. On one hole, they will take it outside to in and on the next inside to out. Inevitably they wind up totally confused and in more trouble than they were in.

The game doesn't have to be that difficult. Simple changes in the clubhead position and the hands and a minor change in swing for certain shots are all that is needed.

I play a fade when I want the ball to start straight and curve to the right at the end of its trajectory. To play a fade, all you do is open the face of the club slightly and increase the pressure with your left hand and decrease it with your right. This ensures that the right hand will not dominate the follow-through. Now just go ahead and swing.

With the face of the club open, the ball will always start right and move right. You must allow for this by aiming no less than thirty feet to the left of where you want the ball to go. Also, do not expect to fade a ball much with anything more lofted than a 6-iron. The lesser the loft, the easier it is to maneuver the ball. That is why so many club players like the lofted irons—they can't slice them!

Every now and then even the best player will push his drive off to the right and find himself in a situation that requires a shot that continuously curves from left to right—in other words, an intentional slice. The club to select is anything from a 2- to a 5-iron, even though the distance you want the ball to go may be no more than 140 yards.

Again, set the clubface open, and increase the pressure in your left hand while decreasing it in your right. With this shot, we make a minor change in the follow-through. You must prevent the clubhead from closing for as long as possible after the ball is struck. In other words, you must make a long lead of your hands, specifically your left, through to the hole and now allow your right hand to roll over.

This, in combination with the open clubface, will give you a natural slice for which you must aim no less than forty feet left of your intended target. I always pick a tree or something well to the left of where I want the ball to go and allow for the ball coming off to the right of it. Remember, with the clubface open, the ball starts right and moves right.

Shotmaking takes courage, but it's these shots that separate the good player from the run-of-the-mill.

A draw, which starts straight and ends by curving to the left, isn't really a shot with which the club player identifies. He is used to a hook, which constantly curves from right to left. Anytime he draws it he feels a sense of accomplishment. When you get down to the brass tacks, the draw and the hook are really the easiest shots to play.

To draw the ball, simply move your hands forward, and hood the face of the club. When I say "hood," I don't mean "close." When the face is hooded, the club is still square to the intended target, but the loft has been greatly reduced.

The key fundamentals in this shot are grip pressure and tempo. This time, when you address the ball, the right hand should grip slightly harder than the left. With this added pressure, the right hand will dominate at impact and, with the hooded clubface and a natural release of your hands, will produce a draw.

For an intentional hook, you must aim farther right and close the clubface as much as you want the ball to hook. Firm up your right-hand grip, relax your left hand and be very conscious again of making a normal release (letting the right hand roll over the left). Although the face of the club is closed, the ball will always start where your swing plane is initiated. In other words, it will start toward the target with which your feet and upper body are aligned and then hook back in.

When the clubface is either hooded or closed, with so much loft taken off, the ball traps on the bottom of the club at impact. It doesn't run up the face as it does when the face is open. For this reason, the initial trajectory of a draw or hook is always low but always straight.

As I mentioned earlier, with the face open, the ball always starts right and flies right. I am making the point again so you will better understand the use of the various types of spin created by the flight characteristics of these shots.

I have in my repertoire a shot that I use quite a bit on the tour. It's called a floater. Sam Snead is identified with this shot because he uses it so frequently. Younger players in the same group as Sam may often look over to see what club he's hitting and be amazed that it is sometimes two clubs stronger than their selection. Well, it is not that the sixty-two-year-old Snead needs that much club. It's just that he's about to play his floater.

He puts an extremely fluid swing on the ball, almost too slow, and the ball seems to float through the air and, when it hits, hardly moves. The reason is that there is little or no spin on it. It's a great shot to have in the bag when you want the ball to get to the hole on a long green.

Try it. Just take two clubs less than you would normally. For this, as for any variation, grip pressure is important. Hold the club with equal pressure in both hands but with less pressure than you'd use for a normal shot. The clubface should be square, hands slightly ahead. Now just make a very slow, lazy swing, and let the clubhead do the work. You'll like the results.

Jack Nicklaus once said about hitting downwind, "There is nothing worse than a player who throws the ball up in the air and leaves it at the mercy of the wind." That started me thinking, and while playing with Jack, I decided to watch his strategy. Every shot that he had downwind was always punched low. The only exception was if he needed a high shot over bunkers or some other form of trouble that guarded the front of the green.

When you just swing normally and toss the ball up in a wind, there is no real way to gauge how far the ball will run after it lands. The spin on the ball is always affected by the wind, and sometimes it is almost doubled. So Jack's reasoning is worth some heed. When you punch the shot, the ball will have a low trajectory and a lot of forward spin. Even if the wind dies in the middle of your backswing, the ball still will get to the green and with a good deal more accuracy than normal.

To play a punch shot, you must first move the ball back slightly in your stance. For me, that means two inches to the right of my left heel, but that is only because I play everything off my left heel from my driver on down. For you, I would say about two inches right of center would be fine.

Hood the face of the club, and move your hands forward. Grip pressure should be equal in both hands and slightly increased to make sure your swing isn't wristy. This shot is similar to the controlled slice in that you want again to delay the release of your hands. Use about half your normal follow-through, and almost literally point the club at your intended target.

A common mistake on this shot is to move the weight too quickly to the left side (sway), which results in the head moving and the shoulders going across the top. Make sure that your head remains in place, and just let your hands and the clubface do the work. If you want accuracy, this is a good shot to call on.

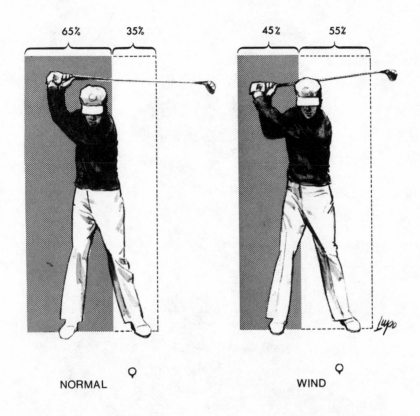

65%   35%   45%   55%

NORMAL   ♀   WIND   ♀

STAY LEFT IN THE WIND

When playing into a very stiff wind, try to minimize your weight transfer to the right side. If your weight is balanced equally at address, transfer no more than 5 percent on the backswing. This will facilitate your move back to the left as well as produce a shot with lower trajectory. Normally, you would shift a bit more weight to the right, say, 15 percent, but against the wind, the same move could lead to your being unable to get your weight back and through the ball. □

BY MAL GALLETTA, JR.

USE YOUR WRISTS FROM HEAVY ROUGH

In every U.S. Open, the rough is tough. There'll be no exception to that rule here at Oakmont, so the boys had better know how to get themselves out of the thick stuff. **You've got to set up with the hands ahead and make the stroke with the wrists.** The club is taken almost straight up by an immediate wrist cock, pauses and then is pulled down toward the ball by a strong leg movement. **At impact, roll the wrists through the ball and heavy grass.** The combination of leg and wrist action will provide the kind of power needed to get the ball out and have it go near the green. □

BY LEW WORSHAM

BLAST IT WITH A 5-WOOD

When confronted with a long shot from heavy rough, don't reach for the long irons. They are too difficult to get through thick grass without snagging. Instead, opt for the 5- or 6-wood, and play the shot as if you were in a bunker, with open stance and clubface. Take the club back a bit upright by breaking the wrists earlier, and hit just behind the ball. Make certain to finish the swing. The ball will pop out, and you will have added a new shot to your repertoire. □

BY BOBBY HEINS

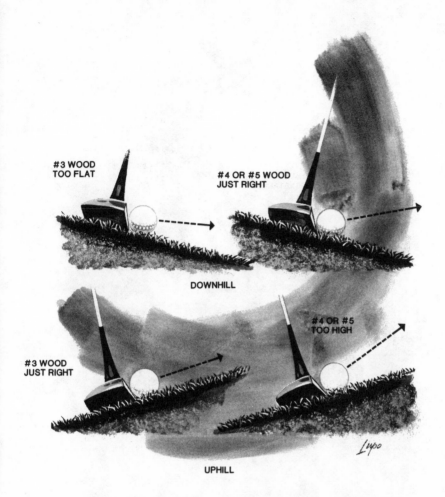

#3 WOOD
TOO FLAT

#4 OR #5 WOOD
JUST RIGHT

DOWNHILL

#3 WOOD
JUST RIGHT

#4 OR #5
TOO HIGH

UPHILL

CERTAIN CLUBS FROM CERTAIN SLOPES

The contour of a sloping lie is going to affect your stance and the lie of the club. **An uphill lie will give extra loft to the shot without your doing anything but hitting it, just as downhill terrain will keep the ball lower.** When you need distance from these sloping lies, you should keep this trajectory problem in mind. From an uphill lie, a 4- or 5-wood will give you height too quickly while a 3-wood will provide just the right trajectory. It's just the opposite on downhill shots, as the 3-wood will keep the ball too low, and the 4- or 5-woods will carry it higher and farther. □

BY CORK CORL

MOVE HANDS DOWN
ON SHAFT SAME DISTANCE
BALL IS ABOVE FEET

ADDRESS FOR
LEVEL AREA

CHOKE DOWN ON UPHILL LIES

A lie with the ball above the feet is one of the most difficult ones for average golfers. They find it hard to maintain balance and make solid ball contact, often hitting behind the ball because no allowance or adjustment is made for the abnormal angle of the terrain. **I've found that by my simply choking down on the grip in proportion to the angle of elevation, a stance can be taken with the feet the normal distance from the ball.** The club can then be swung in the golfer's natural swing plane. Any anxiety the shot normally induces will be overcome, and the swing can be made confidently. □

BY DAVE ROSEN

HIT BALL FIRST

HANDS AHEAD FOR BERMUDA

If you're not familiar with Florida courses, courses that have a sandy subsoil sown with Bermuda grass, it's likely you'll run into problems. If you hit the least bit behind the ball, the wiry Bermuda grass affords no cushion to the clubhead, and the ball will be hit "heavy." To ensure that the ball is taken first, I position my hands well ahead of the ball at the address and consciously hit down at the back of the ball. This results in a shot with low trajectory, good distance and plenty of backspin. □

BY JOE O'ROURKE

59

WEIGHT ON
LEFT SIDE

BALL IN CENTER
OF STANCE

PUNCH IT HOME

You've been there before. You're about 100 yards from an open green, but an overhanging tree limb prevents you from hitting your normal short iron. To hit the shot low under the limb, position the ball in the middle of your stance—no farther back—and keep the majority of your weight on the left side to eliminate any sway. At no time should the hands go above the height of your shoulders. Swing at a steady tempo, and as you hit through the ball, keep the back of the left hand facing the target. Land the ball ten yards in front of the green. The low trajectory of the shot will add the necessary ten yards of roll. □

BY JOHN MARSCHALL

TALLER STANCE

CHOKE UP
ON CLUB

WET AREA

SWEEP IT CLEAN

Lupo

AVOIDING WET FAIRWAY FLYERS

When the fairways are wet, hitting down on the ball with a full swing can lead to errant shots—squirters, as they are sometimes called, because of the water and wet grass that get between the ball and the clubface. It's a better percentage play to use one more club and hit the ball cleanly. What you want to do is hit the ball at the exact bottom of your downswing with more of a sweeping path to the clubhead. The key to this shot is the address position. **Choke up slightly on the club, move the ball two or three inches closer to your body and stand taller over it.** Keep the swing smooth and easy, and you'll find you're throwing the ball right at the hole. □

BY RON CERRUDO

62

CLEAR AREA
AROUND FEET

DO NOT
GROUND CLUB

HITTING OFF PINE NEEDLES

Playing a shot off pine needles can be troublesome to visitors who stray from the fairway in Pinehurst country. There are two things to remember that should be helpful. **First, be sure you're well anchored in your stance.** Clear some of the needles away from your feet, if you can do it without disturbing the ball, because your feet will slip on the needles if you don't have firm footing. **Secondly, don't ground the club behind the ball.** The needles always seem to be in a crisscross pattern that causes a chain reaction when touched, and you're liable to move the ball and incur a penalty stroke. You can hit down and through the ball, though, just as in the fairway. □

BY BOB BRUNO

63

DIG IN

SWEEP IT CLEAN

SANDY ROUGH

When you get in sandy rough, the main point to remember is: Don't be a hero. Getting the ball back on the fairway should be your first consideration. If the ball is lying down in the sand, then you're going to have to explode it as you would a trap shot, entering the sand a little behind the ball. If you have a good lie and need distance, forget about the 3-wood and 2-iron—it's too easy to cold top the shot from this sort of lie. Use a 4-wood or 5-wood, if you have one. On these longer shots simply sweep the ball off, catching it as cleanly as possible. If you have a medium or short iron shot to the green, you needn't change your ball position; simply emphasize a slightly quicker pickup of the club going back, and hit down and through the ball. Grip a little more firmly on this shot especially with the left hand, and if you have to dig your feet in the sand to get a firm footing, choke down on the club to compensate. □

BY MACK McCARLEY

CLOVER LIES

The first thing to remember when faced with a clover lie is: Don't sweep the ball. If you do, too much clover will be mashed in between the clubface and the ball at impact: The result is a ball that flies erratically, like a knuckle-ball pitch in baseball. Instead, you want to descend as sharply as you can on the ball to avoid as much of the clover as you can. You do this by playing the ball back in your stance a couple of inches, setting your weight a bit more on your left side than usual and breaking the wrists a little earlier in the backswing. Even though you make every effort to strike the back of the ball cleanly, some clover will usually be between the clubface and ball at impact. So the ball will fly farther than usual. Compensate by selecting one club weaker than you would normally use for the distance. When faced with a long shot from clover, always go with a wood in preference to a long iron. The wood will spread the clover out of the way, whereas an iron will always cut through, giving a greasy impact. □

BY JERRY FISHER

66

EARLY
WRIST
BREAK

WEIGHT
ON
LEFT
SIDE

PLAY BALL
BACK

CLOVER

70%
WEIGHT
ON
RIGHT
SIDE

OPEN FACE

OVER A TREE

With a short shot over a tree to the green, you play it very much as though you were in a bunker. With about 70 percent of the weight on the right side and a very slight shoulder turn, the arc of your swing will tend to be more elliptical than normal. You should take an open stance with your feet, belt buckle and shoulders aligned left. Open the clubface; this will automatically increase the amount of loft and diminish the distance potential. Position the ball up front, off your left toe. Take the club back normally about a three-quarter swing, and release a bit early on the forward swing. If the shot is fifty yards or less, I recommend using a sand wedge. If it is a greater distance, move to the pitching wedge or another lofted club. □

BY JERRY COATS

HARD PAN

70

HITTING FROM HARDPAN

The key to playing a ball off hardpan is not to try to change your swing too much. Just keep your hands way ahead of the ball when you set up. This could even come in the form of a forward press. Play the ball a bit right of center, and take a normal swing. The stance is square; the clubhead is square to the target. Concentrate on leading with a firm left side. The most common fault among amateur golfers on this type of shot is a flipping out, or breakdown, of the hands at impact. If you set up with the left hand ahead, bowed a bit at the target, the result will be a sharply descending blow, and the follow-through will be natural. □

BY RALPH MORGAN

71

DIVOT HOLES

When confronted with a ball lying in a divot hole, most weekend golfers run scared. They play the ball forward in their stance and try to scoop the ball out. The result is a skulled or fat shot. Instead, I recommend playing the ball back a little so that the clubface is slightly hooded. Then put a normal swing on the ball. Remember, hooding the club reduces its effective loft. So as a general rule, you can forget about using a 3-wood or a long iron. Use a 4- or 5-wood from the better lies where you need distance. From deep divot holes choose nothing less lofted than a 5-iron. □

BY LES FRISINGER

THE WATER BLAST

Think twice before ever hitting a ball out of water. If you have a fairly good lie and half the ball is visible above the waterline, you may decide to take your chances. Use a pitching wedge, and play the shot just as one from high rough forty or more yards away from the target. Take an open stance, break the wrists early and explode the ball out, making sure you hit it with a sharply descending blow. There is very little weight shift and thus an almost negligible amount of follow-through on this shot. □

BY JOHN BUCZEK

4

CORRECTING THE FAULT

by Harvey Penick

When golfers have grooved efficient swings, yet run into occasional difficulty, I am reluctant to make major corrections in their actions. This is particularly true if there is a tournament or club championship scheduled within the next week or so, because a major correction, like major surgery, is apt to be more painful just after the operation than in the weeks to come.

Instead, I will often prescribe some "aspirin" for my patients, quick, simple, easy-to-apply corrections that remove the pain and allow the golfer to regain his or her confidence.

Each of the "aspirin" I am going to talk about here has been tested on thousands of my golf pupils, who come in all shapes, sizes and handicaps.

The reason they work is that I don't correct an error with another error. The "aspirin," as you will see, are rooted in the fundamentals of golf. All of them are based on the fundamental causes of all golf shots: the path of the club, the angle of the clubface and the speed of the clubhead.

For the shanks, or "laterals," as I prefer to call them, the first thing I recommend is to close the clubface ... even to exaggerate it. It is almost impossible to shank with a closed clubface. Now lay your golf bag down on the far side of the ball, two or three inches forward, and parallel to the intended line of flight.

Then go ahead and swing, and I will bet that you can't do it without hitting the bag. However, keep on swinging until you can hit the ball and miss the golf bag. Soon that will be the end of the shanks, the most dreaded disease in golf.

When you are on the course, simply draw a mental picture of yourself hitting the ball on the toe of the club. Really try to hit the ball on the toe as you swing. That will soon get you striking solidly again.

When you have trouble getting your shots up in the air, the problem is most likely that you have been banging down too steeply on the ball, and if this becomes exaggerated, you cannot get the ball up at all. To cure the "lows," you have to think in terms of catching the ball at the bottom of the arc with a more "horizontal" path to the club through the ball than what you've been giving it. And the best way to do that is to think of clipping the grass where the ball is, just as if you were swinging a weed cutter. Think of clipping that grass off under the ball, and you will get exactly the right descending path of the clubhead through the ball to get it up.

All the great pros at one time or another have battled a bad hook. I helped Rik Massengale correct his hook just before a tournament by having him hold firmly with the little and ring fingers of his left hand, both at the top of the backswing and on the follow-through. If you hook, try that.

If your hook is a big "left to left," or if you have had it a long time, then maybe you need to go a step farther. Try this "aspirin": Before you grip the club, set the clubface down a little open at address. Without letting the clubface move, take your normal grip, and square up the clubface. Look at your grip. What you have done is weakened your grip, and this will help you correct your hook.

Actually, for correcting a slice, a principle similar to that for correcting a hook applies. For the slice you will want to strengthen your grip instead of weakening it. Before you take your grip, set the club down behind the ball a little closed. Then take your normal grip. Again, you can check on what you have done by squaring the clubface to the line of flight. Do it. You will see that in fact you have strengthened your grip and that should correct your slice. As with the hook, if the first amount you close the clubface doesn't rid you of the slice, increase the amount; you open it up until the slice is gone.

Here is another "aspirin" for slicers. Use plenty of loft. Until you can hit your 3-wood with a little hook, leave the driver in your bag. It's tempting to reach for the big club, I know, but it also is a whole lot easier to slice with a driver than with a more lofted wood.

Now for alignment problems. If you suspect that alignment may be causing you problems, here are a couple of ways to check, which are a little out of the ordinary.

Instead of putting a club down on a line with your toes, hang the club across the front of your thighs. You may have your feet aligned perfectly—squared to the line of flight—but if your hips or shoulders have turned or your knees aren't bent the same amount, you still would be aligned incorrectly.

Take your address position. Another way to check your foot alignment is to place a ball down both at the toe and the heel of each foot. Then step out from the ball, back to where I teach, which is directly behind the line of your intended shot. Many of you are going to find that you are very open. Several different poor shots can result from that alignment.

Topping the ball is common among beginning golfers and weekend players. Too many golfers try to help the ball up when they should be trying to hit down, while others, in attempting to keep their heads down, either hit the ground behind the ball or rise up and top or even whiff it.

One way to erase this problem, and I have to credit my friend Victor East for this one, is to think of hitting under a table which is a few feet away from you, rather than trying to hit over it. Another one is to be used when you are out on the practice ground. You put your golf bag down a few feet in front of you. Now hit a chip shot with a 7-iron, and try to hit over your golf bag.

Once you have got the idea with a chip shot, you can start hitting full shots with your 7-iron. After thirty minutes or so of this practice, you will have the feel of "hitting down" to get the ball up so thoroughly ingrained into your system that you won't make the mistake of "helping" the ball up again.

GET THE RIGHT BALL POSITION

If you're plagued by shots that fly too high and too short, and also hit a lot of pushed shots and snap-hooks, then it's likely you're playing the ball too forward in your stance. In many cases the reason for the faulty ball position is that you've turned your head to the left at address owing to a dominant right eye. The correction is simple: Cock your head to the right, as Jack Nicklaus does. The correct ball position, more in the middle of the stance, will then become a more natural one. □

BY SUSIE BERNING

CHIN UP FOR
SHOULDER FREEDOM

CHIN LOWERED
BLOCKS SHOULDER
TURN

CHIN UP—EYES DOWN

Too much of a good thing can be harmful, and keeping the head "down" is a good example. A lot of players will overdo this and force the chin into the chest at address. This blocks the path of the left shoulder and forces the swing to be stopped abruptly or the golfer to sway in order to create a longer arc. **What you want to do is keep your head *still*, your eyes on the ball and your chin up or away from your body, so that the left shoulder can pass under it freely.** □

BY CAPT. GENE MIRANDA

79

TEE

TWO TEES CAN BE BETTER THAN ONE

Many golfers have a bad habit of lifting the club too soon in the takeaway or yanking inside too soon. Both these faults can be corrected by practicing with a second tee. Place it four or five inches behind the ball, and push it into the ground so that only the top is visible. When you hit your tee shot, concentrate on sweeping the club back over the top of the tee. This not only ensures a straight, low takeaway but increases the arc of your swing. □

BY EDDIE MUSTY

TREE IT UP TO AVOID A SWAY

Everyone knows it's important to keep your head steady while hitting a golf ball. Unfortunately it's hard to tell when you're failing to do so. One easy way to discover whether your head is "floating" during the swing is to ask a friend to watch you hit some shots as you stand directly in front of a tree. If your head moves past the tree trunk on your backswing, you are swaying. To avoid this, concentrate on feeling your weight transfer to the inside of your right foot as you swing back. □

BY HAROLD "RAGS" RAGLAND

RESTRICTED TURN

FULL TURN

Lupo

DON'T FORGET THE HIPS

Hip movement is an important and frequently neglected element in the start of the golf swing. Too often golfers take back the club only with their arms and shoulders. This invariably results in an overly vertical swing and an outside-in cut across the ball, causing either a slice or a pull. At the start of the swing you should *let your hips turn with your shoulders.* This will enable you to bring the club back and up to its proper position at the top of the swing, with your hands just over your right shoulder. ☐

BY MIKE SAUNDERS

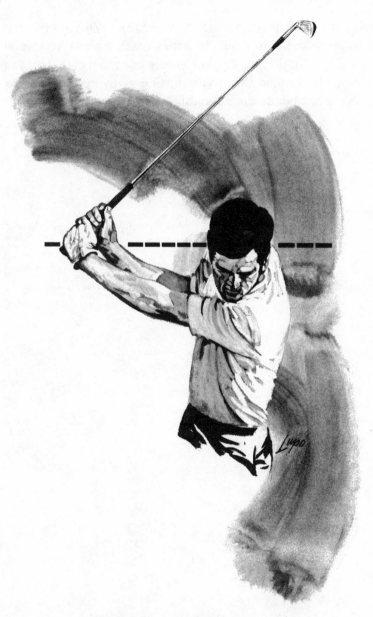

CONSISTENT IRON PLAY

I think the biggest fault the average player has is overswinging with the irons. It's accuracy that counts with these clubs, not whether you can hit a wedge 130 yards. To achieve accuracy and consistency, modify your approach. A three-quarter technique is the easiest to handle and will produce the best results. **With every iron, the backswing should stop when the hands reach a point horizontal with the head.** You might find yourself hitting one more club than you used to, but you'll also find that you're hitting many more greens because your swing has better timing and better rhythm. □

BY DON PADGETT II

ROLL THE DICE FOR PROPER HAND ACTION

I'm often asked how the hands should work in the follow-through. Most weekend golfers think that pronation of the hands requires a conscious roll of the right hand over the left. The result is either a hook or a snap-hook. To encourage the correct hand action, I have the student develop an image of throwing dice onto a crap table with his left hand. Thus, the tendency to overuse the right hand is diminished, and the player's hands work properly, with the left hand in control all the time. □

BY FRED HADDICK

BOX OUT YOUR SLICE

When I find that a pupil is swinging from outside-in, cutting across the ball, I use a simple, effective remedy. I take a cardboard box—a golf club shipping carton is ideal—and set it on the ground at a slight angle to the line of flight. If the pupil swings inside-out, as he should, he will not hit the box. If he swings outside-in, he'll hit the box, knock it flying and have to set it up again. It is not long before the pupil is consistently swinging on the right path. □

BY POWERS McLEAN.

MISS THE EGG TO CURE A SHANK

Once a player shanks, he becomes afraid that it will happen again and again.

To restore confidence, I have a little gimmick that I show members at my club who have a shanking problem. I have them address the ball in the center of the clubface. Then, approximately a half inch from the toe of the club, I place an uncooked egg. Since a shank is often caused by the clubhead's looping across on an outside-in path, so that the hosel contacts the ball first, the problem is corrected immediately. The pupil realizes, subconsciously, that the only way he can miss the egg is to approach from the inside. This he does, and the ball is struck solidly every time. □

BY CRAIG SHANKLAND

VISUALIZE
PITCHING
RUBBER

THINK PITCHING RUBBER

At the start of my swing, I imagine that my right foot is braced against a pitching rubber. This stops me from swaying by keeping my weight planted on the inside of my right foot. Then to start my downswing, I imagine I'm pushing off the rubber, just as if I were throwing a baseball pitch. This gives me added thrust into my downswing. Good weight transference can mean the difference between playing good golf and settling for mediocre golf. By thinking "pitching rubber," you can easily achieve the former. □

BY HANK VERGI

89

A GUIDE TO PROPER KNEE ACTION

If you're plagued with pulling your shots to the left, you're probably turning instead of sliding your hips. Improper knee action as you start your downswing is generally the fault. This causes you to cut across the line rather than to hit down the line of flight. **When I find myself pulling, I practice short pitch shots with someone holding a club lightly in front of my right knee and behind my left.** This makes me slide my knees and hips on the downswing—not turn—and I soon get my shots back in the groove and straight for the hole. □

BY MARILYNN SMITH

90

SLICERS: DROP YOUR HANDS

Slices result when the clubhead comes into the ball from the outside. This out-to-in swing path often is the result of a shoving out of the right shoulder in the downswing. To eliminate that shoving action, start your downswing by dropping your hands toward your right knee. When you do this, your right shoulder stays in the groove, and you can come into impact from the inside, which is the proper path of the swing. □

BY JACK WEINGART

EXTEND CLUB FACE FULLY
TOWARD TARGET

CREATE FULL EXTENSION THROUGH THE BALL

Most weekenders are "quitters." They tense up in the impact area and fail to keep accelerating the club through the ball and on to a high finish. The good golfer gets the club as far away from his body as possible after impact. An easy way to achieve this is to be conscious of this extension while you swing. **Try to "throw" the club past the ball and out toward the target rather than lock your mind in on impact.** You've got to do more than hit the ball; you've got to hit it toward a target. □

BY GARY PLAYER

RESTRICTED
TURN

NO
KNEE
ACTION

FULL
TURN

FULL
KNEE
ACTION

Lupo

RELEASE THE RIGHT LEG

If you finish a full swing with some of your weight still on your right foot, then you're suffering from a very common swing ailment—no release of the right leg. With a locked right leg, you lose a tremendous amount of power because you haven't shifted your weight through the ball and onto your left foot. It's similar to a pitcher who doesn't let his right foot come off the rubber; he loses his fastball in a hurry. At the same time that you swing the arms down from the top, your right knee must move to point at the ball at impact and move on until it points at the target in the finish. The arms and the right leg must work together for maximum power. □

BY MIKE WELLS

WATCH YOURSELF TAKE A DIVOT

One of the causes of topping is lifting the left side on the forward swing. A way to make sure you do not "look up" is to allow your right shoulder to pass your head, keeping your eye on the divot at impact. ☐

BY CARL McMILLAN

LEFT ARM
FULLY EXTENDED

RIGHT ARM RELAXED AT SIDE

CURB YOUR AGGRESSION

Though it may surprise you, a mid-season slice is often a result of your getting more confidence in your swing. As your swing gets grooved, you have a tendency to get more aggressive off the tee, and at some point along the way the aggression turns to hitting from the top. You keep trying for more and more distance, and pretty soon you're releasing the right hand too quickly on the downswing. To prevent or correct this, **take your practice swings with the left hand only—leave the right hand off the club altogether.** This will train your left hand to control the swing, effectively slow your swing down and develop good extension of the left arm through the impact zone. Incidentally, don't be afraid to try hitting some balls this way on the practice tee. It will train you to pull into the ball with the left hand. □

BY BOB HAWER

BY THE NUMBERS

Inconsistency plagues the average golfer more than anything else. So what does he do after hitting a few bad shots? He alters his swing. Instead, he should review his fundamentals, using a full-length mirror and concentrating on the four vital checkpoints. He then can compare his swing with that of a pro who has the same physical characteristics. By the numbers, analyze: (1) address, with the knees slightly flexed, the club an extension of the left arm; (2) at the top, a smooth, full shoulder turn with the left shoulder coming under the chin; (3) at impact, the lateral shift of the legs, the pulling of the left arm as the body returns to almost the same position it was at address; and (4) a full finish with the hands high and the torso facing the target. □

BY LOU SKOVRON

99

5

SHORT GAME

Although you may use any of the more lofted irons around the green, the pitching wedge is probably the most versatile club in your bag. Simply by making basic changes in the position of your hands at address, you can vary the height of your shots, apply backspin to make the ball stop quickly or apply overspin to make it run more.

Sometimes you will want to keep the ball down lower, maybe because of a hard green or because you are playing a windy coastal course. Take an open stance, with the feet and hips pointing to the left. Now all you have to do is to move your hands forward over your left knee. This automatically hoods the clubhead, or delofts it. Then take a normal backswing, and think of letting the back of your left hand stay slightly in front, leading the clubface out toward the target in a square position. The amount of backswing, obviously, is determined by the length of the shot.

You can teach yourself to gauge the backswing and the follow-through only by practice, extensive trial and error. But whatever you do, you should not alter your swing, change the plane, become wristy or use excessive hand action just because you are faced with less than a full shot.

If you want to keep the ball in the air a bit longer and get less roll, as you will if you are playing on the East Coast or any of the lush courses of the Midwest, where there isn't much of a wind factor, you might even want to land the ball right at the base of the flag. All that is necessary is to move your hands back level with your belt buckle, thus increasing the loft of the club. Make the same sweet swing,

101

concentrating on good rhythm and tempo, and again allow the back of your left hand to be your guide. The ball will just pop right up.

There are a couple of mistakes that the average player seems to make consistently. One is that he has his hands too close to his body when he sets up to the ball, and the other is that he often opts for the sand wedge, a much more difficult club to control, when his situation and talent actually call for a pitching wedge.

Having the hands too close is the principal cause of the shank, or the shot that goes flying off the hosel at a right angle. What happens here is that when the hands are tucked in so close and have to avoid the right hip in the backswing, they are forced into an unnatural swing plane in the downswing.

Now for the pitching wedge versus the sand wedge. Well, obviously, if you were out farther than sixty yards, you would have to go to the pitching club. It is stronger, having less loft, and does not offer the resistance of the flange or the bounce of a sand iron.

But now comes the question of the thirty- to sixty-yard shot, the one where the average club player reaches for his sand wedge and decides to go all out, thinking he will land the ball softly and hold the green. Or maybe it's a chip shot, a tight pin placement with the flag tucked behind a bunker. For the amateur the choice seems to be automatic—the sand wedge. The weekend golfer really does himself a disservice in this respect. He would be much better off opting for the pitching wedge and gripping down on the club.

You will see the pros do this all the time. Ben Hogan favored the pitching wedge anytime there was an alternative, sometimes using it even in the sand traps.

Gripping down on it is not a cop-out, as a lot of weekend duffers would have you believe. They honestly believe that if they take the pitching club and club down, it classifies them as a hacker. Well, Lee Trevino puts it this way: "Here's one fella who grips down on the club to get more control and more backspin on the ball. Sure, there are times when I need to carry the ball a certain distance, with height and backspin, and the only club that will do the job is the pitching wedge. Rather than take the chance that I will get too much height, I'll grip down on the shaft and make the same changes to hit the ball high or low, just as I would on a full shot."

The selection of a club for chipping allows for more flexibility. In recent years there have been differences of opinion on whether a player should favor one club as a "chipper" or vary his selection depending on the shot called for. This is a matter of personal preference.

It's the stroke that counts, and one of the more important factors to remember in chipping is that it requires little body action. You might be off the green, some sixty to seventy feet away. Yet you still should try to treat the shot much as if you were on the putting surface, taking into account the condition of the green and its contours.

You should set up with the majority of your weight on the left side, grip the club a little more tightly than normal, choke down for control, shortening the arc and enabling you to hit the ball a bit more crisply. The fact that you are holding the club firmly will minimize the wrist cock and give you an evenly paced swing with no jerkiness. You control the hit solely with your arms and hands. Never try to lift or scoop the ball. Allow the loft on the club to perform this.

There is no doubt that high handicappers give away far too many strokes from ninety yards in. The short game means work, but the time you devote to practice can pay handsome dividends. And it is an area of the game where physical strength or lithe young bodies do not have any particular advantage.

JUDGING WEDGE-SHOT SWING LENGTH

On wedge shots from thirty to ninety yards, the average player has trouble judging how much backswing is needed to supply sufficient force. My advice is to follow through first with a practice swing and see how high the hands must go before they obstruct your view of the top of the flag, the cup or the spot on the green on which you want the ball to land. From thirty to forty yards, you'd want to pick a spot; from forty to sixty yards, your target would be the cup; and from sixty yards out, the top of the flag is your aiming point. **The height your hands require to cover this aiming point is the height your backswing should achieve.** This little visual aid also gives you good target projection for the actual swing at the ball. □

BY DICK COSTELLO

FOLLOW
THROUGH
FIRST

105

HEAD
STEADY

BACKSWING
NO HIGHER
THAN
FOLLOW
THROUGH

CLUBHEAD
POINTS TO
TARGET

WEIGHT ON
LEFT SIDE

THE COMPACT WEDGE SHOT

Since the pitching wedge is used primarily for short shots, it's only
logical that the swing should be short and compact. To set up firmly,
place most of your weight on the left side, open your stance and grip
the club firmly with the last three fingers of the left hand. The swing
itself should have little or no body movement and is made with the
arms rather than the wrists. **To complete your compact package, keep
the backswing and follow-through the same length.** That length is
dictated, of course, by the length of the shot. □

BY HOWARD ARCHER

106

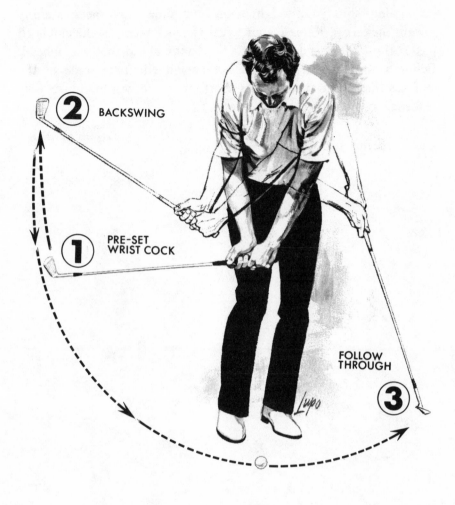

PRE-SET YOUR WRISTS FOR BETTER PITCHES

For more consistent pitches in the ten- to forty-yard range, try this unorthodox, yet reliable method. Pre-set your wrist cock *before* you start your backswing, and maintain that set position throughout the backswing and into the impact area. Here's how: After you address the ball in your usual way, raise your club to an almost horizontal position simply by cocking your wrists. With the wrists thus cocked, begin your swing by turning your shoulders and body slightly. On the downswing, shift your weight a bit, and slide your knees laterally toward the target. Release your wrists (uncock them) as the clubhead passes through impact, keeping your hands ahead of the clubhead. Follow through naturally. This action will eliminate some of the stiffness that often accompanies short shots and will minimize your tendency to scuff, or blade, the ball. □

BY BOB BENNING

CLUB FACE
REMAINS OPEN

OPEN FACE

FAST
WRIST SNAP
THROUGH IMPACT

SHARP DOWNSWING

BALL OFF LEFT FOOT

HOW TO PITCH IT HIGH

When the pin placement is just over a trap on a plateau, a high, soft shot is required—one that gets up quickly and stops just as fast. To make this shot, play the ball off the left foot, open the face of your wedge as you would in a sand trap and make a sharp downward stroke. **Snap the wrists quickly through the impact area, and let the clubface stay open on the follow-through.** This will work for any pitch up to about eighty yards, depending on the length of your backswing and follow-through. □

BY PADDY SKERRITT

109

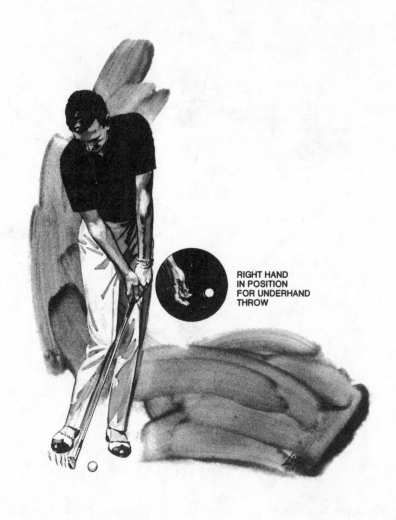

RIGHT HAND
IN POSITION
FOR UNDERHAND
THROW

UNDERHAND THE PITCH SHOT

There are certain images I try to maintain in my mind throughout the season to prevent me from falling into bad habits. One of the most useful, and most successful, is the underhand pitch. Much like a thrown softball, **the golf ball will go where the hands guide it on shots that require little or no body motion.** The short wedge pitch shot, say, from seventy yards in, is just such a shot, and I try to imagine myself throwing it underhand with my right hand. This keeps my right palm going at the hole and makes sure I get good extension toward the target on the follow-through. I let the left hand lead and release the right hand at precisely the moment I'd release a softball, just after the hand reaches the bottom of its arc. □

BY CHARLIE GRIGGS

"BUMP" BALL
INTO HILLSIDE

BUMP AND RUN BEATS THE WEDGE

When you're faced with a pitch over a mound to a tight pin placement, do you instinctively reach for the wedge? **I've found much more success with the "bump and run" chip that hits into the upslope, bounces over the crest and rolls down the other side onto the green.** By being hit into the near side of the hill, the ball trickles nicely down the slope and frees me from worrying about hitting the wedge too hard, a worry that often leads to a dubbed shot. I like to use a 6- or 7-iron for this shot, the 7 if the downslope is steep, the 6-iron if it's a gradual incline. ☐

BY PAM HIGGINS

112

1 TO 5 FEET
OFF GREEN
USE 3-4-5
IRON

15 TO 20 FEET
OFF GREEN
USE 7-8-9 IRON

DIFFERENT CLUBS FOR DIFFERENT SHORT SHOTS

A lot of golfers suffer mid-season chipping lapses simply because they fall into the habit of pulling out the same club to do every type of job. It's a form of carelessness developed because of spring successes with a certain club. You need to remind yourself that each club in the bag is designed to handle a specific assignment. **When you're faced with a**

113

chip from the fringe, you should use the 3-, 4- or 5-iron to produce a chip that is as close to resembling a putt as possible. **When you've got twenty or thirty feet between you and the green, the more lofted 7-, 8- and 9-irons are more desirable** because they'll loft the ball over the fringe grass and land it softly on the green. You'll have to allow for plenty of roll on the 3-, 4- and 5-irons, but toss those short irons about halfway to the flag. □

BY GERRY LA VERGNE

HEAD ALMOST DIRECTLY OVER BALL

SNUGGLE UP TO THOSE CHIP SHOTS

For more consistent results on short approach shots, snuggle up to the ball as you address it. First, move in close to the ball with your toes about eight to ten inches from it. Secondly, narrow your stance so that your feet are less than a foot apart. Thirdly, flex your knees and bend forward at the waist. Finally, keep your arms close to your body.

If you now find yourself looking almost straight down on the ball,

115

you'll know that you've snuggled up correctly. Remember, reduce your body movement to a minimum while executing the stroke from this position. You'll be amazed at the consistency you'll achieve in your short game. □

BY DR. RICHARD MACKEY

TURN THE LEFT HAND UNDER

The most common mistake the average golfer makes in chipping is allowing the right hand to pass the left too quickly. The only successful way to chip is to have the ball hit the green and roll, not bounce, to the cup. This can be accomplished only by your leading the

117

entire shot with the left hand. **Curl the left hand under a little on the takeaway, and leave it in this position as you pull the club through the ball.** You'll hit the ball firmer and straighter. □

ELIMINATE YOUR WRISTS

To be consistent with shots around the green, it is essential to develop
an action that is firm—in other words, one that employs very little
wrist movement. Unfortunately the tendency among average players
is to slap at the ball only with wrists, using no shoulder and arm
action. To teach my students the importance of a firm action, I use

the device you see illustrated. Although this isn't available to you, the concept is easily remembered. Next time you practice your chipping, imagine your right hand is on another club behind the left. Your shoulders will rotate, your arms and hands will follow their lead and you will thus eliminate that wristy action that destroys many a player's short game. □

BY JIMMY CORRIGAN

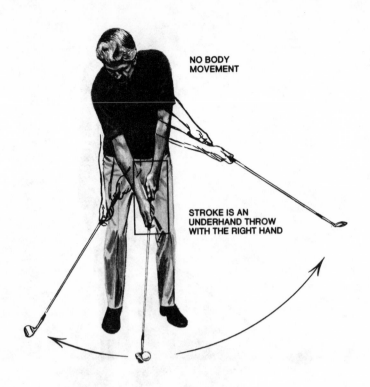

NO BODY MOVEMENT

STROKE IS AN UNDERHAND THROW WITH THE RIGHT HAND

SEPARATE HANDS FOR MORE CONSISTENT CHIP

The short chip shot is one of the most delicate and demanding shots in the game. You can't be satisfied with merely getting on the putting surface; you want to get that ball up there within one-putt range, or the shot has not been successful. With this kind of pressure involved, most golfers have a tendency to be unsure of themselves when it comes to length of backswing and follow-through. I've found that separating the hands on the club is a great aid to those troubled by this type of shot. **By placing the right hand at the bottom of the grip, while the left hand remains in its normal position at the top of the grip, the golfer gets the feeling that he is throwing the ball underhand to the hole.** There is no body movement needed, and the right hand picks the ball and gets it rolling straight at the cup. □

BY JOE LISS

121

THE SOFT CHIP

The soft chip is the right shot for those delicate downhill situations when you need to get the ball moving without much forward roll. Stand with your feet close together, your left shoulder elevated, and keep your right hand relaxed. Use a sand wedge, and open the face. **Hold the club lightly, and make the stroke by hinging and unhinging the left hand.** The result is a brief pendulum stroke which pops the ball in the air and drops it softly on the green. If you wear a watch on your left wrist, the face of the watch should be looking at the target from start to finish of this little stroke. □

BY DON KAY

6

SAND

Average players make bunker play such a complex matter. The swing they use in the sand does not come close to the swing they use off the fairway into a green. The first rule of good sand play is to keep the swing as close to the normal as possible, regardless of the lie.

There is no need for a fancy wrist break in the takeaway and no need for a drastic deviation from the normal swing plane. Any changes should be purely fundamental—in other words, in the address position. Beyond these changes it is a matter of understanding such things as the length of follow-through for short and long shots. You restrict your follow-through for a short shot to about waist height. For a long shot your hands carry the club up to a high finish, about the same as you would use on a normal iron shot. In any case, the backswing length never changes.

An understanding of how much force to use in different situations also is extremely important. This can come only through practicing. From practice you also gain understanding of what happens to the ball when, for example, you open, square or close the clubface. With the clubface open, you can expect the ball to fly higher and for less distance and to stop quickly. Square, the ball will fly slightly lower and longer and will run a little more. With the clubface closed, you will have no backspin, a low trajectory and a lot of forward roll.

Your lie in the bunker will not always be a good one, so you must develop an understanding of how the ball will react in various situations and the compensations to make.

But first, let us get down to the basics. The first thing, once you are over the ball, is to dig your feet well down into the sand to form a secure base for your swing. Good balance is imperative. Your stance should be slightly open, with the ball positioned just inside your left heel. Choke up on the club. Your weight should favor the left side, and your hands should be slightly ahead of the ball to help you initiate the swing smoothly. Aim for a spot in the sand one and a half to two inches behind the ball.

Now the key—tempo. Sam Snead and Julius Boros, two of the finest trap players in the game, have something in common: long and very slow backswings. The slower you swing, the easier it is to coordinate your movement. The longer you swing, the more time you have to gauge distance and gain that all-important feel.

Next, let us look at the different situations you will face on the course, starting with the uphill lie. From an uphill lie, the ball naturally flies much higher. To compensate, you must use more force—hit harder—in your follow-through. First, though, remember to dig in your feet. If you sink in after your swing starts, you will hit behind the ball and leave it in the bunker.

Try as much as possible to make the plane of your swing match the contour of the sand. You can accomplish this by setting your weight back on your right side. Your follow-through will be restricted by the steepness of the slope and can cause you to quit on the shot or to stop just after impact. To compensate, take a firmer grip on the club, allow for some jarring in your hands and make a conscious effort to lead through the ball with your hands as far as possible.

The natural tendency with most players in handling an uphill lie is to leave the shot too short of the hole because of the height and lack of force they use in their swing. Do not be short; always try to get the ball past the hole!

If the ball is under the lip of the bunker, the same fundamentals apply as for the uphill lie. However, because you need additional height on the shot to get over the lip, you must turn the clubface wide open. Instead of setting your hands slightly ahead of the ball in your address, move them back, level with the ball. Moving your hands back will allow your right hand to work under your left to a greater extent, thus producing additional height on the shot. The farther ahead your hands are, the lower the trajectory will be.

In this difficult situation, the common error is to hit fat, taking too

124

much sand; this results in the ball's barely making it over the lip and then getting stuck in the fringe of the bunker. This happens because the player fails to get enough weight back on his right side to assist him in hitting up through the slope and because, as with the uphill shot, there is not enough force applied in the downswing.

Regarding a downhill lie, you also will want to make the plane of your swing match, as much as possible, the contour of the bunker. To help accomplish this, kick your right knee in toward your left. This will set most of your weight over on your left side, while it sets your body at right angles to the slope.

Because of the downhill slope, the ball will, if you have the club only slightly open, have a low trajectory, so open the clubface a little more. Remember first to dig your feet well into the sand.

In the actual execution, even if you have to move forward laterally, you must hit down; otherwise, you will catch the ball rather than the sand and hit the shot thin. Be conscious of hitting down through the sand with your hands leading.

On a sidehill lie, when the ball is above your feet, never let the clubface turn over or close. The fact that the ball is above your feet makes you swing flatter; this causes the ball to go to the left. Your first compensation, therefore, must be to align yourself well to the right of the target. Your instinct will tell you the ball is going to go left. You can prevent it going farther left by weakening your right-hand position on the club.

You also must choke up on the club a little more. If necessary, go all the way to the bottom of the grip. This will ensure that you do not dig down too deeply into the sand, a common error in hitting the ball on a sidehill lie. You will find that the sand offers about the same restriction to the clubhead's path as a normal bunker shot, so less force is required, and more finesse. Above all, keep the overall action slow, long and smooth.

When you are faced with a downhill lie where the ball is below your feet, the ball will have a tendency to travel to the right (the opposite of an uphill lie). You must, therefore, start by aligning farther left of the pin.

There is a tremendous danger, with the ball below you, of skulling or at least hitting the ball thinly. You must grip up on the shaft of the club; the amount depends on the severity of the slope. Also, stand as close to the ball as possible. Flex your legs, and keep your knees at the same flex throughout the swing. This shot requires more finesse and smoothness than force.

In a plugged lie there is no possible way to get backspin on the ball, and you must allow for a lot of roll. Move the ball back in your stance. Set your hands ahead of the ball, creating a steeper downswing arc. This is essential to help you get down under the depression in which the ball sits. Your stance is open with the ball back, opposite the right heel.

Make a slow shoulder turn, and hit down and through the ball. As a result of the depth the club travels under the ball, you can expect your follow-through to be somewhat restricted. This does not mean that you need to make a gorilla swing to get the ball out. Too much force is the most common error. In fact, little force is required. The closed clubface is going to do all the work for you.

PLAY THE SAND SHOT BEFORE YOU HIT IT

My blasting into the cup to win the Sealy LPGA Classic was, of course, partly due to luck, but luck only comes to those who help create it. Before I step into any trap, I try to review exactly what I'm going to try to do once I get over the ball. **I always stand off to the side of the trap and pick a spot in the grass to represent the ball.** Aiming two inches or so behind that spot, I take a smooth practice swing, being sure to follow through. I take the turf just as I'll take the sand when I make the actual shot. Then, without delay, but without hurrying, I walk into the trap, step up to the ball and dig my feet in slightly. **Without stopping to think and freeze, I look at the hole and repeat my practice swing.** This gets me onto the green every time before fear can grab me and make me force the shot. □

BY SANDRA PALMER

ADDRESS THE SPOT

When faced with an explosion shot from the bunker, don't make the mistake of addressing the ball. A simpler and more effective method of extricating yourself is to position your body so that the spot behind the ball, or target, is at the low point in the swing. By mentally excluding the ball from the picture, you will be more likely to execute a good bunker shot consistently. □

BY NELSON LONG

CLUBHEAD
POINTS
TO SKY

Lupo

WEIGHT
ON LEFT
SIDE

CLUBHEAD'S UP

When confronted with a sand shot, keep in mind you are going to have to hinge your wrists very quickly on the takeaway. Take a firm footing, with most of your weight on the left side, the ball off your left heel. Open your stance a bit, and allow the clubhead to swing back with the toe pointing toward the sky when it's waist high. This "pickup" type of action will help guard against smothered shots, and the sharp angle of descent will get the ball up softly on the putting surface. □

BY TONY JACKSON

FOOT LINE

CLUB PATH

BALL PATH

"X"ING OUT OF THE SAND

If you're having difficulty with sand shots around the green, try making a mental picture of an "X" when you set up over the ball. Draw a mental line from the ball to the target, and then imagine a line crossing it exactly at the ball. This secondary line should be aiming at a point twenty feet to the left of the ball line. Now set your feet parallel to the second line. **The ball line is the flight direction of the ball; the secondary line is the path of the club in the swing.** □

BY PAUL KELLY

131

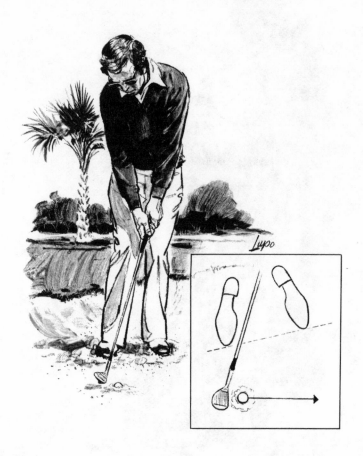

BURIED LIES MADE EASY

Too many golfers think that they have to bull their way out of a partially buried lie. In reality, you don't have to swing any harder than you would on a ball in a good lie. You have to make only a couple of adjustments. First, use a pitching wedge instead of a sand wedge. The pitching wedge is better suited to cutting down into the sand. Secondly, instead of opening the face of the club as you would on a sand shot from a good lie, square the leading edge to your target. This also will help you to dig the ball out and will avoid the need to swing any harder than normal. □

BY TOM WAGNER

NORMAL

FOR LONGER HIT

NORMAL

FOR LONGER HIT

STEP BACK FOR THE LONG TRAP SHOT

One of the most troublesome shots in the game to the average player is the long trap shot from around the green. From forty or fifty feet, he's indecisive as to how much sand to take and how hard to swing. **The answer is to stand a little farther away from the ball.** By reaching slightly, the club will automatically make a shallower path through the sand, and you don't have to force the swing. □

BY BILLY ZIOBRO

MOVE IT BACK IN FAIRWAY TRAPS

Here's a quick tip for those of you who have trouble getting your iron shots out of fairway traps the way you'd like to. You know you've got to hit the ball first, and there are two ways to make sure you do it. **Play the ball back in your stance off the right toe, and then hit down and through.** The ball will travel on a low trajectory but will have plenty of spin once it hits the green. Just be sure you have a club with enough loft to clear the bunker lip. □

BY DUB PAGAN

134

7

PUTTING

Putting technique probably is the most widely discussed subject in golf, and with good reason. There is no one "correct" way to putt. There are few hard-and-fast rules. Some of the best putters the world has ever seen, players such as Bobby Locke and Billy Casper, were strictly wrist putters in their heydays; champions such as Jack Nicklaus and Tom Watson effectively lock their wrists and execute the shot with their arms and shoulders. Gary Player successfully jabbed at putts for years before altering his style and winning the 1978 Masters.

Putting, then, is an individual matter and could even be dictated by emotional makeup, according to Harvey Penick, acknowledged as one of the better teachers. "It takes steadier nerves for that good, long stroke. A nervous individual can't putt that way," contends Penick. "He tends to have, or maybe should have, a short, snappy stroke."

But although putting is dependent on the intangible property of feel, there are certain fundamentals one should attempt to incorporate into one's game.

Regardless of which variety of grip you use, the position of the right hand should be stronger or turned more under the shaft on the putter than for any full shot, including a chip shot. This will inhibit the right hand from rolling over and turning the shot off line.

Although you should attempt to use the same grip consistently, grip pressure will vary with the length of the putt. Some players hold the club tighter on short putts; this means they take their hands and fingers completely out of the stroke. However, the grip need not be any tighter than is necessary for one to control the club.

If you have trouble lining up, walk up to the ball from behind, glance at the putter blade, put the blade down square to the line and take your stance. The blade often looks crooked because you look at it so much from above and thus lose some perspective on the angle. So program your putts by pre-setting the putter.

At address your eyes should be directly over the ball. Although you may be somewhat inside the ball or behind it, like Nicklaus, you should never allow yourself to lean so far forward that you are looking back at the ball. This makes it even more difficult to determine if the blade is square. Play the ball off the left heel, or even the left toe, because the farther to the right you play the ball, the higher the backstroke will have to be, and if you are high on the backstroke, you are going to hit the ball with a descending blow. Try to make the length of the follow-through match the length of the backstroke.

Now, when it comes to the actual stroke, many players and teachers alike believe there should be no movement of the lower body. There are some, however, who believe that this restriction causes the player to tense up and become rigid over the ball, lessening the feel factor. All we can conclude is that there should be a minimum of body movement.

The action itself should feel like an underhanded movement of the right hand, with the palm of the right hand going directly at the cup. The feeling has been likened on more than one occasion to that experienced when you pitch pennies: obviously you attempt to land the ball as close to the hole as possible.

Putting is the one area of the golf swing where the right hand dominates the action, allowing for a pendulumlike motion. This would not be the case if the left hand were to dominate, since it would inhibit the takeaway motion and turn the face of the putter off-line.

Start the stroke with a small forward press, and let the putter swing back low along the ground. Then let the clubhead swing back through the ball without your hands trying to force it with a steering motion. A very wristy putter will simply allow his wrists to unhinge, and the club will pull his hands back to impact, whereas a shoulder and arm advocate will keep his left wrist firm while moving it at the hole. There is no conscious manipulation of the putter blade.

On shorter putts you should concentrate more on the line than distance, while the opposite is true of longer putts. If you practice enough, your muscles will tell you how hard to hit the ball. Most poor putters will come up short on small putts, and there is no explanation other than the fact that they did not hit the ball squarely or make solid contact. One way to see if you are hitting the ball on the sweet spot is to put some chalk on the back of the ball, and, after putting, to check the blade to see where you are catching it.

Again, there are two schools of thought on breaking putts. Many players putt to a spot, while others advocate visualizing the entire roll or curve of the putt. Do not depend on a caddie to give you the line. Only you know how hard you are going to hit the ball, and since speed is very important as to how the ball will break, only one person can determine the correct approach. Also, do not delay over a putt or agonize with it. Once you have made your decision, go with it. It is the only way to build confidence.

And the mental side of putting is probably underestimated. Once you "know" you can roll the ball into the hole, that is more than half the battle. Ben Crenshaw, after a particularly good putting round, once said, "I felt as though I could just will the ball in."

Anyone who wants to pay the price can become a good putter. The price is many hours on the putting green: many putts analyzed, faults corrected, priorities altered, confidence built.

To revive an old adage: The best way to putt is the way you putt best. And the only way to determine this is through practice. Confidence will come as a matter of course once you have started sinking putts with any regularity.

Harvey Penick once said, "You have faith first and then confidence. If a pupil believes what I teach him, or even believes in what he has learned himself, and works on it, it won't be long until he has gained the mental boost."

Although Ben Hogan once remarked that the three most important shots in golf were the drive, the chip and then the putt, the order could be reversed for the average golfer, who loses far too many strokes around the greens.

LOCK WRISTS FOR SQUARE-BLADE PUTTING

I've been a staunch advocate of the "locked wrist" putting technique for thirty years. While there is an infinite variety of putting techniques, and though this one feels quite awkward initially, it will pay stroke-saving dividends on the greens, because **it takes out of the stroke unnecessary "play" in the hands.**

To assume the proper locked position, turn both hands outward so that the palms face the sky. Place the left thumb down the left side of the shaft, and the right thumb down the right side. Use either the overlapping or reverse-overlapping grip, whichever feels more natural. **With this lock, there's little possibility of the putter blade's opening or shutting owing to rolling hands.** This is the key to good putting—keeping the blade square back from, to and through the ball on the target line. □

BY JOHN THOREN

138

SQUARE UP

Most golfers know the importance of square alignment. They're also aware of the "two-club" setup that teaches the feel of what is square. But these same golfers practice with this alignment aid only on full shots. I disagree with their thinking. First, it's much easier to learn alignment on a short stroke than on a full swing. Secondly, what you learn about alignment in putting carries over into your long game. Thirdly, correct alignment is crucial in putting—you can recover from a missed drive, but never from a missed putt. □

BY JOYCE KAZMIERSKI

LEFT TOE IN, HANDS TOGETHER

Good putting stems from a minimum of movement, and that's why I recommend the following two points. First, to lock your body into place, **take a wide stance, and turn your left toe in to point at the ball.** This will firm up your legs and keep your body still. Secondly, unify your hands by placing them with the palms directly opposite each other. **Hold the club in the fingertips of the right hand, and then place the first two fingers of the left hand over the fingers of the right hand.** The last two fingers of the left hand hold the club lightly, and the tip of the index finger touches the shaft. This will tie the hands together, yet leave enough sensitivity to allow for "touch." □

BY GARY GROH

LET YOUR RIGHT HAND HIT THE PUTT

When I come across a student who has trouble keeping his putts on line, I ask him to grip the putter so that both the palm of his right hand and the blade of the putter are facing the target. Then I ask him simply to swing his right hand back and through, using a stiff-wristed stroke. By keeping the right palm and the blade parallel and swinging that right hand, he soon starts rolling the ball straight. □

BY WALT CAMPBELL

AIM FOR THE MIDDLE
OF THE BACK OF THE CUP

POP THE SHORT PUTT

There's no point in lagging one from two feet, although I see many golfers do just that. They try to steer or guide the ball into the cup from close range and wind up hitting it weakly. The only way to attack a short one is to step up and "pop" it right into the back of the cup. No nonsense, just a firm rap. **If you hit square for the back middle of the cup, there's no way for it to veer off line within the short distance it has to travel.** If you hit it weakly, you're just as likely to push it or pull it as to leave it short. □

BY KEN VENTURI

144

FIRM STROKE ON DEW-COVERED GREENS

When Mother Nature blankets the greens with early-morning dew, two changes must be made in putting strategy:

1. The stroke must be firmer to ensure that the ball gets through the moisture and up to the hole.

2. The breaking distance of the putt must be halved because the dew on the surface of the grass will prevent the ball from following the natural contour of the green.

These two simple rules will rid you of those early three-putt greens. □

BY TOM GALICANO

TRY WATCHING THE CUP

If you're unhappy with your putting, try this unconventional method. Look at the cup as you stroke the ball. Watching the target may seem like an outlandish idea, but remember that in certain sports, such as basketball, hockey and bowling, you always keep your eyes on the target.

Settle into your stance; then lock your eyes on the cup. In so doing, you will also lock yourself into a secure position. With your eyes on the hole instead of the ball, you won't be tempted to move your head as you take the putter back. The results are a steadier stroke and greater accuracy on all lengths of putts. □

BY RICHIE BASSETT

PATH FOR
INSIDE-OUT
STROKE

KEEP PUTTER ON THE PENDULUM PATH

The most important factor in a successful putting stroke is the pendulum path of the club. This is what produces true overspin and keeps the ball on line. To teach yourself this inside-out pendulum action, set up two rows of tees when you practice on the putting green next time. Since you must keep the blade low to ensure good contact, add another tee about three to four inches behind the ball. **Now firm up your left-hand grip, loosen your right hand and keep the putter moving within the confines of your "tee track."** You'll notice immediately that when you knock over the tee behind the ball and don't dislodge any of the barrier tees, your ball will have perfect roll. Work with this principle for ten minutes before every round, and watch those scores come down. □

BY TOM TAGGART

PRACTICE-PUTT A TENNIS BALL

If you never practice-putt with anything but a golf ball, you may develop a stroke that is too low to the ground. This can cause you to hit the ball below center, imparting backspin and an undesirable *sliding* rather than *rolling* action. **To develop a true rolling action, practice-putt with a tennis ball.** Try to hit it above center. You can readily see, because of its larger diameter, when it starts off with a definite roll. You'll be surprised at your improved accuracy, especially on spike-marked or rough greens, where the ball must *roll* as much as possible. □

BY DON COPELAND

PUT IT IN THE HOLE

One of the most common errors my pupils make when faced with a short putt is to tighten up so much that they jerk the putt left of the hole. To overcome this, I tell them to imagine they are putting the clubhead into the hole on the follow-through. This simple mental image prevents jabbing and assures them that the ball will follow the intended line. It has another plus going for it in that it keeps the ball rolling and overcomes any tendency to leave those vital putts short. □

BY ERNIE RIZZIO

USING THE FLAGSTICK

The flagstick can provide a great practice putting aid while you're waiting for those farther from the hole to putt. Get off to the side of the green, and **swing your putter blade just above the flagstick.** You'll straighten your stroke out immediately! Incidentally, while you're waiting to hit in the fairway, any club in your bag will serve the same function. □

BY FRANK PURCELL

8

MENTAL APPROACH

Your hands perspire. Your knees turn to jelly. Your normally steady putting touch becomes shaky, and your drives streak into the sand traps and water hazards. In short, your game is going to pot. And so are you.

It's really a matter of nerves, the downhill spiral of stress causing a physical breakdown, which, in turn, makes the situation even more stressful. And the trigger is the improper mental approach. You choke because you think about choking, about the consequences of missing a short putt or shanking a wedge shot.

The way to stop this type of performance is to free your thoughts from the negative subjects and focus them on something productive and positive. Channel your concentration; direct your thoughts in a way that will melt away the tension.

Begin at home by preparing a game plan. It's similar to the pre-game planning of football coaches on the days before their next game. They study the strengths and weaknesses of their opponent. And so should you. Analyze the golf course's difficult and easy holes, and determine a winning strategy (fading the drive at Number 3; hitting a high iron to the seventeenth green; using a short putting stroke for the course's slick-as-glass greens).

Before playing the course, play it in your mind. Visualize every shot, and go over and over all eighteen holes until you can play them perfectly in your mind. Do this the night before you play and again in the morning, while you drive to the course, to reinforce your focus.

Essentially, this is a mental exercise geared to give you a physical advantage. Start by visualizing the course you will be playing. If it is unfamiliar, concentrate on those positive aspects of previous rounds on other new courses where you've made superb shots and dropped putts for birdies or pars.

If you know the course, you should picture in your mind precisely where you want to position each ball on each hole. See every type of shot you could be called on to make—with every club.

The next step is to look at your swing. Stand in front of a full-length mirror, and watch yourself swing. Better yet, have someone shoot home movies of you hitting balls on a practice range, or go to a golf professional who has videotape equipment. Seeing your swing for the first time can create a negative response, like hearing your voice on a tape recorder for the first time, so make sure you look for the positive aspects as well. Then memorize them so you can visualize your best swing at any time.

Even if you cannot see your golf swing, you can picture proper timing and rhythm by visualizing an ideal golf swing, such as Sam Snead's. With strong, concentrated visualization, you can actually hear the swish of the club and the click at impact.

Analyzing the mechanics of the swing and pre-game planning can make the actual play easier. You'll be reacting instinctively to circumstances with which you already are familiar in your mind, rather than dwelling on the basics, thereby making your swing fluid and automatic.

Once you get to the course, allow time for a few mental exercises before you begin your round. Start by taking a few practice swings with your eyes closed. This should heighten your awareness of what your body is doing. If you aren't swinging properly, you will fall off-balance. But stick with it, and within a few minutes your tempo should improve and your swing should become consistent.

Next, select a target on the range where you want the ball to land. Pick a personal swing key, such as a leg movement. Make three to five mental swings to "feel" the leg movement. Now step up to the ball, and execute the shot, with your attention keyed to the leg movement. Repeat this three to five times.

If your initial results are not good, don't dismay. This is a proved approach for ingraining the key movements so that on the course your swing will flow. And you can review five or six keys in this fashion before teeing off.

Another mental exercise is to visualize the perfect shot. Stand behind a practice ball, and conjure up the ideal swing. Picture the ball soaring through the air and landing smack on target. Repeat this at least three times.

Now step into the address position, and focus on a target. Look down at the ball, but hold in your mind a picture of the target. Then glance back at the target to make sure it is just in the spot where you thought it was.

If it seems to have "moved," focus your attention on it more carefully to determine its precise location and distance. Now repeat the process of looking from the ball to the target at least three times. When the target is ingrained in your mind, look at the ball again, and execute the swing. The final glimpse of the ball should be for only a fraction of a second because the longer you stare at the ball, the more likely it is your picture of the target will fade. Also, tension is liable to creep in at this point.

The same technique should be followed on the putting green. Putting practice should consist of more than hitting a couple of quick twenty-footers and then charging off to the first tee.

What is accomplished by this pre-round series of mental exercises? First, your concentration is heightened. Your swing motion is more automatic. And in many instances, you may find you are not conscious of your swing because your attention is shifted from your body to your target.

When a golfer has had a superb round of golf, he often will say he has played "out of his mind." In reality, he has played "out of his body." His thoughts were undoubtedly focused on his targets rather than on the mechanics of his swing.

Your success on the course also should improve if you focus your concentration. For instance, analyze the lie. Determine the exact target; observe the distance; consider the wind and other environmental factors. Allow your past experiences to help dictate the best shot you can hit under the existing conditions.

Then visualize your shot. Picture the swing, hear the click and imagine the ball zooming right to the target. If you are attempting to fade or draw a shot around trees or bunkers, see the imaginary trajectory. Visualize the ball curving around the obstacle and rolling to a stop. And do this until, like Jack Nicklaus, you can say you never have hit a bad shot—in your head.

While you are still behind the ball, observe your grip and make any necessary adjustments. That way your attention will not be diverted from the target when you address the ball. Then take a practice swing at 75 or 90 percent of your full speed, and visualize that you've just hit the ball along the ideal path.

Now address the ball. When you look down at the ball, do not move your body, but be aware of the target's location. Then look back at the target to make any necessary movements of feet and shoulders for better alignment. When you are comfortable with your position, rivet your attention on the target once more so that it is clear in your mind when you look at the ball. Once your eyes have shifted back to the ball, swing immediately. If this routine is followed on every shot you hit, including putts, your concentration will improve immensely.

Selecting targets on the course also is a mental art, one that will develop your powers of concentration further. And targeting on a golf course is similar to aiming a rifle at a range target. Each hole has its bull's-eye, the cup, which is surrounded by a larger ring, the green. It may seem elemental, but it's often overlooked.

As you stand on the tee, your attention is invariably drawn to the water hazard, the grove of trees on the left, the out-of-bounds fence on the right and the clusters of sand traps. These diversions can cause you to miss the target just as easily as if you tried to hit a bull's-eye with a rifle from 200 yards while looking somewhere else. Instead, pick out the details of the target. Implant in your mind the color of the flag, the quadrant of the green in which the cup is.

The average golfer will simply hit the ball and hope it lands in the fairway. Yet the same golfer will often take extra time to hit a ball through a small opening in a bunch of trees. He will aim his shot and mentally see it fly through the hole without being aware of it. Use the same approach when hitting the tee shot. Aim for a target, a small knoll perhaps, rather than just anywhere in the middle.

These mental exercises of aiming and visualizing will not improve your game overnight. It takes time and practice to develop a routine, to channel your thoughts. But once you do, you'll find your shots are more accurate and your hands don't perspire.

DON'T FIGHT YOUR NATURAL TENDENCY

There are many players who don't have the time to correct a hooking or slicing problem. These players should turn the problem into an asset by understanding it, then using it on the course. My suggestion starts at the driving range. Pick a target, a bush, tree or yardage marker, and count the number of shots hit to the right and the number hit to the left of it. You will then find not only your natural tendency but also the approximate distance to allow for it on the course. ☐

BY ROGER GINSBERG

160

THE LONGER DRIVER

Through the years many fine amateurs and professionals, especially smaller and senior players, have gone to a slightly longer club to get that distance they might lose from age or lack of size. It all comes to this: You can gain greater distance by increasing clubhead speed or by increasing arc. **Increasing arc is taken care of for you by the longer club.** Instead of being harder to control, the swing is easier, and you don't have to alter your swing pattern if you don't exceed forty-five inches. And don't think for a moment that a lot of touring pros aren't using longer clubs. □

BY GENE LITTLER

READ THE TREES CAREFULLY

Using trees to judge distance is a good idea—if you know how to do it correctly. I classify trees into two groups. The first is the palm type, the tall tree whose long trunk reaches high before any branches begin to grow. With this type of tree, do not focus on those lofty branches. You'll be adding the height of the tree to the distance, and you'll overclub. Look instead at the base of the tree if you want a truly accurate reading.

The other type of tree is the thick, bushy one. Here, beware of the tendency to look at the closest branches. You will invariably err on the weak side. Again, look at the base of the tree. Then pull out the proper stick. □

BY BILL KEHOE

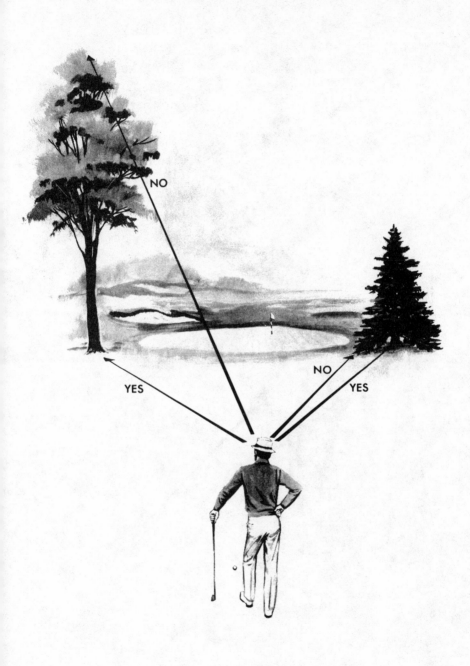

163

HIT THE "TARGET"

The average player gets so wrapped up in the mechanics of his swing that he often forgets that golf is a "target" game and that the whole point of a target is to set up your next shot. For example, on the dogleg par five illustrated you should pick the point that will avoid trouble and enable you to hit to the next target, the point which gives you a sure shot into the green. If you always think "target" and plot your targets with the next shot in mind, you'll always play a good percentage game. □

BY DICK KOLLAR

HIT IT ON THE LABEL

A lot of you probably don't know this, but you're costing yourself ten to fifteen yards every once in a while just by haphazardly teeing the ball. Hitting the ball on its seam means hitting it at its weakest part, and this can lead to loss of both distance and accuracy. **Always tee the ball with the letters at the point where you want to make contact.** It'll help you to keep your eye on the spot for impact and give you more distance and consistency. □

BY LEE TREVINO

HIT THE LETTERS

168

USE YOUR BEST SHOT

Many amateurs find difficulty visualizing a shot before they play it. They've been told to visualize the desired swing, the desired trajectory of the ball and the sphere hitting the target. But when they try these things, they often fail. If this is your problem, try to remember the best shot you've hit recently with the same club you're playing. You'll be surprised how sharp is your visualization, and this clear image can program a fine shot. □

BY TOMMY DEBELLIS

169

WALK THE LAST
FEW YARDS TO
THE BALL

LET YOUR CART HELP YOUR SCORES

To speed up play, some resorts such as ours [Las Vegas] require powered carts for all golfers. If you're a cart user, here is a tip that will help improve your game. Always take turns with your partner on the driving. When it's your turn to get off, do so a few yards before you get to the ball. This will give you time to loosen up and think out the shot you'll be playing next. It will also give you a chance to clear your mind of that nongolfing chat you may have had in the cart. □

BY PRESTON YOUNG

3-IRON   5-IRON   7-IRON   9-IRON

BEGINNERS: TEE IT UP FOR CONFIDENCE

Without wishing to offend those who believe in strict adherence to the rules, I sincerely believe that a lot of beginners, especially the ladies and juniors, would be better off if they teed up every shot while they're learning the game. This eliminates that frustrating period of topping and lets the beginner develop good swing habits rather than try to lift the ball into the air. The tees should be higher for the woods and low irons and work their way to being almost ground level for the 9-iron. In practice sessions, he or she should alternate hitting with and without a tee to develop confidence in getting the ball up either way. Believe me, it doesn't hurt their games, and it gives them a chance to concentrate on the swings. □

BY DAVE BARON

9
EXERCISE AND PRACTICE

Although the average golfer rarely gets the opportunity to play more than once a week, there are things he can do in the interim to help improve his game. In this chapter we are going to deal with some of the exercises specifically aimed at developing the golfing muscles as well as the formulation of a productive practice program.

Before we get into what is good and bad, as far as exercises are concerned, let us make some observations. Most people take stock of their physical condition at some point, because of something they have read or something they have seen in the mirror, and resolve to make themselves physically fit. Then they cut down on cigarette smoking a bit, possibly even start jogging or working out at a local gym. This usually lasts about three weeks or so. Then the cigarette intake is back up again, the television is more important than the jogging and the gym becomes "too crowded."

It does not help to start something and not finish it. For an exercise program, and a practice regimen as well, to be beneficial, it must be maintained over a period of time. Unless one makes a strong mental commitment to "get in shape," nothing outlined in this chapter will be of any benefit.

Although some of the following exercises do require special equipment, for the most part all that is necessary is a willing body and mind. Most of them can be done within the confines of your home.

Of course, the single best exercise is the act of swinging a golf club. It will help you develop a rhythm, coordination and feel. If you are anxious to improve your power potential, the best way to accomplish this is to weight the clubhead. This will help strengthen the wrists and arms as well as discourage the practice of hitting from the top.

Many younger men make the mistake of thinking that a weight-lifting program will help improve their long game. This is not necessarily the case, because power is not the sum of your muscles but a product of their suppleness. This is true of golf or any other sport that requires timing and coordination. Big, overdeveloped muscles actually are harmful in playing golf. Golf requires a resilient strength, like a volcano, ready to erupt from within when needed.

Heavy weights, especially when used to develop the muscles of the biceps and chest, can be detrimental to the smooth swinging action necessary to play good golf. That means no curls, no presses and definitely no bench presses. If you are determined to use heavy weights and have a gym at your disposal, do leg builders. You can use as much as but not more than 250 pounds, if you put the bar across your shoulders and do toe raises or half squats. Do not attempt the full squat. This does nothing but contribute to knee injuries.

We would suggest that if you are serious about staying in shape during the week or even over the winter, the best pieces of equipment you could obtain are a fifteen-pound dumbbell and a spring stretching device. On trips, where you might not want to carry the dumbbell, the hand squeezer or even a sponge rubber ball can help you attain the same results.

Actually, the only other item you need is a pair of running shoes or sneakers because the leg muscles are probably the most neglected part of the anatomy. Running of some kind is basic to the development of your golf muscles.

Now let us take it step by step. To strengthen the hands and wrists, simply take the sponge rubber ball qr a hand squeezing device, and press it tightly closed. Hold it this way for seven seconds before you release it. Now squeeze again. Alternate hands as you do this exercise. The more often you are able to work with the "squeeze," the better. If you are scheduled to take an airplane flight or are riding in the car or commuting on the train, don't feel embarrassed to exercise your hands. It will pay off.

For the legs, we have already mentioned half squats and toe raises with heavy weights across the shoulders. However, although the effort may be a lot greater in these exercises, there is nothing to substitute for running . . . or even walking.

Running is the single best exercise there is. You don't have to try to set any records; merely attempt to keep a consistent pace with deep, regular breathing. You can supplement your running program with variations of jump-squats. Kangaroo jumps are a good example. Stand on your toes, squat down and jump as high as possible into the air. Since most of us live under a nine- or ten-foot ceiling, try to touch it with your fingertips. Do this ten or fifteen times, twice a day.

Another excellent leg exercise requires the use of a wall. Simulate a sitting position with your back pressed against the wall, your arms dangling at your sides and your feet spread shoulder width. Hold this position for one minute at first. Later, attempt to maintain this position for two minutes.

As a last leg exercise, there is the one-legged squat. Although this might be difficult at first, there is a definite reward for perseverance because not only will this help develop your leg muscles, but it also will teach you a sense of balance. Just hold one leg out in front of you a few inches off the ground. Now do a knee bend on the other leg with your arms outstretched to help you maintain your balance.

To help in the development of the forearms and wrists, work with that fifteen-pound dumbbell. Hold one in each hand at arm's length and at shoulder height. Rotate the wrists clockwise for ten seconds and then counterclockwise for ten seconds. If you do not have access to a dumbbell, merely extend your arms and do the same thing, doubling the amount of time. Remember, don't bend your arms, or you will lose the entire effect.

But once more, there is no exercise for the golfer which can pay the dividends of either swing or simulating a golfing action. For example, take the hand squeezer, and swing into the impact position by pulling with the left hand while resisting with the right. Then push with the right hand and resist with the left. If you do not have the squeezer, do it by placing your palms together and allowing them to work against each other. You can also go through the motions of the golf swing with a weighted bar or dumbbell. The stress should be placed on the pulling action of the left hand. So do some swings only with the left hand. Try to keep the arm firm and fully extended as you swing the weight back slowly to the top of the backswing. All these exercises teach the muscles to work correctly and provide a good swing groove which you will be able to put into practice on the golf course.

But there also are some mental calisthenics which cannot be eliminated from this exercise program. First, anytime you go for a walk, you can practice judging distances by pacing off certain segments. Before going to bed at night, you can pick up an iron and write your name in the air a few times, just to acquaint yourself better with the feel of the clubhead. One more routine, this one in the area of eye-hand coordination, is simply to take an iron and bounce a ball on the same spot about thirty or fifty times without dropping it.

Now suppose you do get an afternoon or two during the week that you want to devote to the improvement of your golf game. Many people foolishly waste their time at driving ranges throughout the country, flailing away at the ball with no idea of what they are trying to accomplish. There is a need for a definite practice program, one which will keep you sharp, allow you an edge, mentally as well as physically.

To do this, you must be able to analyze your game, know the areas where you need the most work and plan your practice time accordingly. Far too many golfers just go out on the practice range and grab either the driver or their favorite club, the one with which they feel most comfortable, when they should be doing just the opposite.

The first thing to do is to make certain you are practicing alone. This will help you avoid any unnecessary distractions or breaks in concentration.

Then allot so much time to the different areas of your game, for example, the driver, fairway woods and long irons, approach shots, pitching and chipping or putting. The easiest way to accomplish this is to go back over your last few rounds and see where you're weak and strong. If you can't remember, the next time you play, bring a notebook and record your round shot by shot. Note how many fairways you hit, how many greens you reached in regulation, how many good shots hit with each club, how many bad ones, how many of your approaches fell short, how many were long, to the left, to the right.

Determine how many putts you took. How many times were you able to get up and down in two from off the green? How did you play

176

your sand shots? At what point of the round did you feel your game turned sour?

If there is one problem which is predominant in your game, that is the area on which you must work, and you will have to adjust your practice schedule accordingly. However, after every round you should dissect and reflect on the good as well as the bad parts of your game. This is not to say that you should dwell on the negative aspects. Step outside yourself, and be critical in a positive manner. The most important aspect of good practice is not to allow the same mistake to continue rising to the surface.

One way to help avoid this is to practice immediately following your weekend round, while the memories of bad shots still are vivid in your mind. You might even head back out onto the course, if possible, and lay a few balls down, placing yourself in the same situation. This is the time to experiment.

Anytime you practice, whether it be on the practice range, the course or even a driving range, you must establish a target awareness. The target might be a leaf or a clump of grass or an actual practice green. It is just important that you have something to shoot at. There must be a definite focus on distance and direction if the practice session is to be considered productive, and when we speak of distance, we are talking more in the realm of the range of each club rather than how far you can wallop it.

The game of golf is built around the search for consistency, the ability to reproduce shots from like situations under the most tenuous circumstances.

Consequently, a good practice session will be one in which you can go through your entire arsenal, starting with the short irons and working your way up through the driver. The touring pros do this. They also hit a good many partial shots, expending only 35 to 50 percent of their power potential. Take an 8-iron, and try to hit it three different distances; vary the trajectory; work the ball, always with a definite target in mind. This will develop a sense of feel, timing and, ultimately, confidence.

While you are doing this, keep asking yourself what is the correct blade position and path for the particular shot at hand. Where is the ball in your stance? Consistent execution of the shot can come only after complete awareness of the concept.

The best way to accomplish this and have a bit of fun at the same time is to imagine you are playing your home course, visualizing each hole. Hit the drive, the approach. Would you be on the green or pitching up? Go through the entire eighteen holes in this manner. Play the percentage shots. Gamble and go for broke. Experiment. Trial and error, that's how you build a sound golf game.

One note of caution, though, if you do attempt this routine. That is, do not rush your way through. Approach each shot as if you were on the course playing a $10 Nassau. Grip, alignment and address can easily be overlooked in the average player's practice, yet these contribute to more bad shots than anything else.

Work on tempo and rhythm. See just how easily you can hit the ball. Just practice bringing the clubface back to the ball square, making crisp contact. Vary your swing keys, and see what each helps you produce. Attempt to maintain the same pace as though you were playing a round of golf, possibly even walking away after each shot.

Once more, the mental factor cannot be emphasized too much. Visualization is the prime element in one's mentally preparing oneself to play golf. Try to see yourself playing each shot successfully. Visualize the course, and develop a game plan just as a football quarterback might. Allow yourself time to daydream a bit, to envision yourself on the seventy-second hole of the U.S. Open with a one-shot lead and a difficult test facing you.

You must know every hole on the course, attempt to remember previous rounds, all the good shots you have hit under similar conditions. This retentive ability is a large step in your becoming mentally prepared. The positive thinking also helps you keep from becoming intimidated by an exceptionally difficult course. Even more important, once you are mentally tuned, you are better able to analyze the various situations which might confront you, to know the repercussions of a bad shot, and to objectively assess your chances of execution.

Make the most of your time and exercise and practice with some realistic goal in mind, and that is to be as good as you can be. Imitation is beneficial in the young child, but it is not pragmatic for the man of forty years old to think that he is going to begin swinging like a Jack Nicklaus or a Johnny Miller at this stage.

If you are going to attempt to emulate one of the better golfers, choose someone in the same age bracket and with similar physical characteristics.

If you are unable to practice at the golf course during the week, do the exercises, and chip or pitch some shots in your backyard. Get ready. It's almost the weekend.